Teaching
as a
Performing Art

Teaching as a Performing Art

SEYMOUR B. SARASON

Foreword by Maxine Greene

Teachers College, Columbia University
New York and London

Published by Teachers College Press, 1234 Amsterdam Avenue, New York, NY
10027

Library of Congress Cataloging-in-Publication Data

Sarason, Seymour Bernard, 1919–
    Teaching as a performing art / Seymour B. Sarason ; foreword by
Maxine Greene.
      p.   cm.
    Includes bibliographical references (p.).
    ISBN 0-8077-3891-3 (cloth). — ISBN 0-8077-3890-5 (pbk.)
    1. Teaching. 2. Teachers. 3. Performing arts.   I. Title.
LB1025.3.S273   1999
    371.102—dc21   99-34549

ISBN 0-8077-3890-5 (paper)
ISBN 0-8077-3891-3 (cloth)

Printed on acid-free paper
Manufactured in the United States of America

06   05   04   03   02   01   00   99   8   7   6   5   4   3   2   1

To Irma Miller

Beloved by me and
by all who know her

Contents

Foreword

If we were to attempt to write the narrative of Seymour Sarason's professional life, we would find ourselves pursuing themes of great and challenging diversity. They are themes that lead into one another, expand one another, and at length converge. In this book they converge into a rendering of the teaching act that may change our view of life in classrooms and, at once, our grasp of the journeys of particular teachers as they discover what it means to mediate between subject matters and the consciousness of students ready to learn to learn. Not only has Dr. Sarason been able to look through the lenses of disciplines familiar to him: psychology, psychiatry, sociology, and the arts. With his own rich tradition of inquiry into the cultures of public schools, he has been able to bring into startling life what those lenses disclose, especially when it comes to education in each professional field.

Because of his acquaintance with so many fields of study, he enables his reader to enter the worlds of medicine, theatre, music, dance, and what he believes to be the tragically inadequate domains of teacher education. Yes, he recognizes current attempts to call attention to the importance of teacher education. Realizing, however, how many windows remain to be opened, he ushers us into spaces new to us in his effort to clarify what he means by teaching as a performing act. He does *not* have in mind a routinized, behaviorist approach to teaching. Drawing from the work of Stanislavsky in theatre, Jersild in psychology, Schaefer-Simmern in the study of artistic activities, Freud, Dewey, Comer, and many others, he enables us to focus on a self-reflective absorption in subject matter along with an authentic, caring interest in moving students to choose to learn.

He makes it possible for us to ponder such transactions and awakenings in differing contexts, thus helping us to put aside what we often take for granted about diverse pedagogies and see our own projects afresh. We are introduced to some of the great practitioners past and present with the enthusiasm of someone who knew them personally or knows their work so well that we find ourselves in a person-to-person (or a mind to mind) relation to them. Indeed, Dr. Sarason may remind us of the passage at the end of Toni Morrison's *Beloved* when Paul D tries to describe his feelings about Sethe: "She is a friend of my mind. She gather me, man. The pieces that I am, she gather them and give them back to me all in the right order. It's good, you know, when you've got a woman who's a friend of your mind." People introduced as colleagues or collaborators or admired teachers are given center stage and we find some of our own cherished certainties transformed.

Dr. Sarason also introduces contemporary works that have moved him or influenced his thinking. He finds instances of passionate thinking or passionate teaching in contemporary films. He introduces his own critical response to a well-known play like *Master Class*, especially as enacted by and even possessed by the actress, Zoe Caldwell. (It will be recalled that the play presented one dimension of teaching, a communication of a way of being and thinking to those desperately eager to learn.) Perhaps best of all we are treated to stories having to do with Dr. Sarason's own experiences in schools and clinics and theatres—backstage and in the audience.

The book invites us to join an ongoing conversation, as we are introduced to all sorts of men and women and young people, all in search of humane purposes, all creating themselves by means of freely chosen projects. En route, we are made privy to friendship, to disagreements and agreements. We feel the presence of children with effective teachers and teachers who have lost hope. We enter classrooms, under Dr. Sarason's guidance, that are veritable examples of "savage inequalities"; and we enter classrooms where, for all the shabby surroundings, empathic teachers are moving children of many cultures to tap their own experience, to write and write. He reprints a child's poem. He speaks of what it can mean when "a shy, abandoned child" bares his soul to those around—and how nothing has ever rivaled "the courage, beauty and humanity of that child."

There is talk about theory and whether it is useful. There is talk of the limitations of school psychology, of Dr. Sarason's failures as well as his successes. Out of lived experience, out of a history of writing about schools and teachers from multiple points of view, Seymour Sarason wants us to think about artistry, even as we reach out to children. He invites us to choose ourselves afresh, to learn from students as we learn from our books, to pay heed, to learn to see what surrounds us—and, yes, to become friends of one another's minds.

Maxine Greene
William F. Russell Professor Emeritus
Teachers College, Columbia University

Preface

The reader may be familiar with the quip that books are not finished, they are abandoned. In the case of this book I can say that I know that it is not finished, if by *finished* is meant that I have covered all the major points in depth and did not neglect the viewpoints of others. That is by way of saying that it was not my intention to write a scholarly treatise, and for several reasons. For one thing, the literature on teachers as performing artists is sparse compared to that concerned with the selection and training of those in the conventional performing arts. The second reason, derived from the first, is that I decided that my focus in this book should be on clarifying several things: Why teaching should be taken seriously as a performing art; why teacher preparatory programs are part of the problem and not of the solution; the resistance that should be expected to a truly radical reconceptualization of the selection and training of teachers; and why some of my concrete proposals will be viewed as impractical or require too long a term time-perspective for those (educators and the political community) possessed of the quick-fix mentality. In this book I have tried to confront each source of resistance and criticism. Needless to say this book will be of little or no interest to those who believe that there is little that is basically wrong or self-defeating in the rationale for the selection and training methods of teacher preparatory programs. Those who think that way are responsible for whatever cosmetic changes have been introduced into these programs over the decades, with the consequence that the more things have changed the more they have remained the same.

I am not the first to say that teaching is a performing art. Over the years of my close work with teachers more than a few of them said, "Teachers are actors. We perform." They did not mean that they were in show business but rather they were the vehicle by which the script (the curriculum) became a source of interest, a personal and intellectual goal to an audience inevitably heterogeneous on many variable-affecting attitudes toward learning. And, as a group, they were refreshingly candid in saying two things:

Their formal training, far from being helpful, was an obstacle they had to try to surmount, and they did not think they had overcome the obstacle in a satisfactory way. As several said, "I am not the actor type. I feel uncomfortable, even hypocritical, when I feel I am putting on an act."

I have long been interested in performing artists: how they self-select themselves for their chosen careers, and the training they receive. It took me a long time to connect what I was learning with what teachers said about themselves as performing artists. It took a long time because I had failed to realize that these teachers had a most superficial understanding of the goals and obligations of actors or of those in other performing arts. I only made the connection in the course of writing *Caring and Compassion in Clinical Practice* (1985), in which I came to realize that I had to include a chapter on teachers in addition to chapters on physicians, psychiatrists, clinical psychologists, and lawyers in family practice. The present book is a lineal descendent of that earlier one.

It is one thing to confront and adjust to the fact that your book is unfinished. I can come to terms with that, especially in light of my advanced age. What will be far more difficult to come to terms with is if it turns out that the issues I raise are ignored by the field.

Anyone who has read my previous books will not be surprised that I take delight in expressing my gratitude to and affection for Lisa Pagliaro, who again was so unfailingly helpful to me.

Seymour B. Sarason
Stratford, CT

Teaching
as a
Performing Art

CHAPTER 1

Some Personal Reflections on a Teaching Career

In 1985 I wrote *Caring and Compassion in Clinical Practice* about physicians, psychiatrists, clinical psychologists, lawyers in family practice, and teachers. The thrust of the book was that preparatory programs for these professionals were far from adequate in ensuring that practitioners understand what is involved in becoming or being caring and compassionate and conveying that understanding to those they sought to help. The last chapter of the book was "The Process of Understanding: The Relevance of Stanislavski for the Clinician." In regard to acting no one more than Stanislavski (1936) has illuminated so well how an actor absorbs or becomes a role that is believable to an audience, even though the person being depicted in the role is markedly different from the actor in "real life." Each of us, every day, interacts with others, and we feel obliged and are expected to convey that we understand what the other person is feeling and why he or she says what they do. And each of us has had the experience in which we conclude that the other person is unable or unwilling to comprehend what we feel or say.

Occasions that compel us to try to understand for the purpose of helping are not frequent. There are occasions that arouse us, mightily so, and cause us to try to understand ourselves and others, but they usually do not lead us to use that understanding to help another person. When they do, however, we become aware that, if arriving at understanding has problematic features, wedding that understanding appropriately to caring and compassionate actions is even more problematic, unless, of course, one confuses intent with desired outcome. The process of understanding does not guarantee desired outcomes. It is a necessary but not sufficient condition for action. Our understanding may be incomplete or faulty—it usually is—but that does not necessarily mean that actions geared to helping will be experienced by others as uncaring or uncompassionate. It is often the case that others sense our desire to be caring and compassionate, and they appreciate our effort, but at the same time they know that our actions fall far short of their mark. What disturbs people, what makes the wall around them seem so impermeable, is their sense that helping actions are powered by the language of social ritual and not by any real grappling with the process of understanding. And that is the point: the process of under-standing is a grappling one that is manifested overtly in ways that say, "I am trying to understand because I want to be helpful." It is those manifes-tations that are experienced as caring and compassionate, even though they may be more or less ineffective. But when they are effective, the helper and helpee are both changed.

We like to see ourselves as caring and compassionate, but people dif-fer dramatically in their ability and willingness to undertake the process of understanding in order to use those feelings for appropriate actions. To want to understand implies a commitment to action whose boundaries are necessarily unclear until one has reached the point where one feels that one understands. If we resist that process, it is in part because we intuitively know that the commitment to action may involve pain or inconvenience or self-sacrifice on our part; that is, we resist the changes within us that understanding and a commitment to action imply. If we are not born with the desire to understand or with caring and compassionate feelings, we are far from comprehending why people come to differ so markedly in these respects.

After I wrote the 1985 book—and mulled over Stanislavski's and Gielgud's introduction—that which should have been obvious to me from personal experience, but was not, was that teachers were performing art-ists. I taught in one university for 45 years. My classes, really seminars, were small, but I had taught for several summers in other universities to very large classes. From reviewing my experiences as a teacher, several things became relevant to performing.

1. I had no formal or informal preparation for teaching. The assump-tion in the university is that if you know your subject matter you will con-vey it adequately to your students. I knew that was self-serving nonsense. After all, I had been a student for 20 years, and if I knew anything, it was that teachers obviously differed in many ways to student reactions and in their style of delivery—from chaotic-rambling to a well-ordered "recita-tion" of facts; from looking at students to random gazing elsewhere; from conveying a sense of personal and intellectual security to a puzzling op-posite sense; from uttering sentences which might have no end or even verbs or any clear connection to previous sentences to an interconnected-ness of sentences and ideas that was exemplary; from a diction that was slurred or could use technological amplification to a clarity and amplitude

that left no one in doubt that they heard what was being said; from appearing to talk as if to one's self to an obvious recognition that there was an audience. Most teachers fell in between these extremes; included here are teachers whom I regarded as performers, but only in the sense that they were intent on impressing students *not* with their teaching ability or impact, but rather with the distinctiveness or uniqueness of their personalities. Yes, they were always "on stage" in a self-glorifying role, they were self-consciously performing. Generally speaking, students may like such performers; at the same time, they may not regard them highly in discharging the obligations of being in the role of teacher.

2. I have never come to a class without experiencing some small or large degree of stage fright. That is related to another fact: I never enter a library without the depressing thought that I will never be able to read all of the books in it, and this long before I ever taught. To me, to be a teacher meant I had to know everything about the subject matter; at the same time, I knew (how well I knew!) that what I knew was far from adequate. Would my students sense this? How to strike a balance between being self-revealing and conveying security about my degree of expertise? How did I want to come across to my audience of students? In the role of teacher I was not in the role of friend, husband, father, poker player, or son. When my parents were alive and I would visit them, I knew that I was not "performing" as an adult, a psychologist, or a professor, but as a son with memories and obligations. Different audiences, different performing styles and goals. What were my goals as teacher? That students should like me? That by words and actions I respected them, that I did not regard them as devoid of assets and experience, that they deserved I should take them seriously, that I seriously sought in diverse ways to know whether the subject matter I was obligated to convey was assimilated, mulled over, and utilizable by them? I had good reason then and now to experience stage fright. I was going to be performing in a role new to me, a role of which I had only been on the receiving end, in the audience. How could I meet their expectations and my obligations in a convincing, believable fashion? A teacher is more than a conduit of subject matter. A teacher literally creates an ambience on the stage of learning and that teacher is the chief actor, the "star," the actor who gets top billing. Some plays close after one performance, some teachers close (lose their audience) after one class. How do you keep them coming back for the right reasons? For all of these questions I was unprepared, and yet I had to figure out how to become someone I had never been before, someone inevitably related but by no means identical to what I "really" or ordinarily was. I felt I would be acting, a feeling that initially I regarded as hypocritical but later came to see as otherwise: the role demands that the teacher performs for the audience. The question is how to

become a convincing, impactful performer. By the time I retired after 45 years of teaching I gave myself a grade of B. That was not undue modesty. I had experienced and learned a lot about teaching and audiences, not the least of which was that resistance to changing one's style of performing the role is the constant enemy of deepening understanding of the role. The burned-out teacher tends to be one whose performance has been routinized, like an actor in a long running play who once "lived" the role but now goes through the motions.

3. In the theater an actor is not given a script and left to his or her own devices to interpret a role. Although in the process of becoming a role the actor is obviously crucial, it is axiomatic that the actor is an imperfect interpretive instrument. That is why there are many rehearsals before the play opens, and that is why there is a director whose main task is to assist the actor to understand, deepen, and enlarge the myriad nuances of the role. Although the actor was preselected because he or she was deemed capable of performing in the role, it is by no means rare that during rehearsals the director or actor (or both) may conclude that the actor is incapable of doing it justice, even if that actor has performed well in previous plays. For the actor each role is or should be a struggle to understand the role, to make it believable to an audience. The written script is like a curriculum, the task of the actor and the director is to make it alive for an audience and that obligation is not discharged by knowing the script, by regurgitating it. Becoming and sustaining a role is an artistic process of identification and imagination about which our comprehension is far from clear. When I became a college teacher there was no one who prepared or stimulated me to think about the teacher as a performer. If, when I began to teach, someone had said that the teacher had notable commonalities with the performing artist, I would have been offended. Actors, I probably would have said, strive to make the imaginary real, but my job is to present and discuss ideas, theories, and what others have studied and reported. My answer would not and did not explain why I was so frequently dissatisfied with how well I was teaching. I was a teacher of "truths," but I was too often impressed that students were not buying them. The temptation to blame the students was always there, just as it is always there for actors who try to explain a play's failure by blaming unappreciative, uncomprehending audiences.

4. What furthered my interest in teacher as performer were the three occasions early on when I taught large classes in the summer. Given what I said about teaching ideas, theories, and a relevant literature, you would think that large classes would not be difficult or intimidating. I could not have been more wrong. What those experiences forced into awareness was that I, like an actor, needed a responsive audience, not one taking notes or passively listening or, as on several occasions, dozing. I did not fully real-

ize how much I needed to see, feel, and react to members of an audience. I would stand at the lectern and lecture, every weekday for 5 or 6 weeks. I think it fair to assume that the students thought I knew the subject matter cold; I could not assume that I had warmed them up. I found myself acting the role of the Olympian professor bringing information to the uninformed. I was not cut out to play that role. I knew there were college instructors who were much acclaimed about the way they play that role, but I also knew that in the bulk of large classes the audience was far from engaged. An actor wants to feel he or she has engaged the audience, that he or she has sparked their imagination, that they will willingly and eagerly come back after intermission and that, highest of all praises, they will buy tickets to see the play again. A teacher, like an actor, wants to have an impact during the performance but both also clearly want that impact to continue in some way to some degree afterward. You perform in the here and now in the hope that your performance has a future in the memories and actions of the audience. Why, after my first experience with large classes, did I do it two more times? The answer is: money and a desire to see different parts of the country, not because I wanted to see what other universities were like or because I loved teaching so much that I was unhappy not teaching for the 3 summer months. I learned the hard way that the strength and source of the motivation to teach very much affects your performance in, enjoyment of, and stimulation from teaching. An actor may say that his or her heart was not in the role just performed, a way of saying that discharging of the obligations of the role was shortchanged. There are many college teachers, especially in our research universities, whose picture of heaven contains only research, not teaching.

I have talked here only about some aspects of my experience as teacher-performer. The fact is that my imagery of teacher as performer in large measure derived from my 12 years as a student in public schools. From all of those years I can recall but three teachers who I felt understood me, and made it safe to ask questions and to acknowledge my concerns about grasping certain ideas and skills. I truly felt they understood me, *wanted* to understand me. Most of my other teachers were nice people, likeable people, but they didn't *engage* me; I learned what they said I needed to learn, but what I learned had little meaning for me, it had no motivating power, it was no spur to thinking, it had no relevance to questions I had, but felt too unsafe to ask. These teachers, in contrast to the three I mentioned earlier, never recognized (or sought to recognize) my individuality. It is as if they took me for granted; I would learn what they said I should learn, even though I did not understand why. I said earlier that I gave myself a *B* as a university teacher. That may be too high because I think I can make a case that I was not much different from the bulk of my public school teachers, although I would like to believe (of course) that I improved somewhat as the years went on.

Over the decades, I have had the opportunity to talk with, observe, and interview hundreds of school teachers as well as many teachers of teachers. What I will say will, I hope, give the reader a basis to understand why I regard teaching as a performing art. My main interest is less in convincing the reader that teaching is a performing art and more in indicating that the process by which a person enters and grows up in the traditional performing arts has enormous implications for improving teaching.

A performing artist is one who uses him or herself to convey an emotion, or situation, or imagery intended to be meaningful and stimulating to an audience. The "message," whatever the medium, is for the purpose of evoking in others the response "I understand and believe what I am seeing and believing. You have not left me cold, you have engaged me." It is an engagement that leads symbolically (and hopefully) to a marriage: artists and audience are *willingly* in a new, reciprocal relationship. In the case of the teacher, engagement is a sustained one; it is not a one-night stand. It is an engagement the basis of which is thinking, learning, attitudes, and feelings, the goal of this indissoluble mix being to experience the warmth and excitement of change and growth. But that goal is easier to state than to implement. Indeed, as I shall discuss in later pages, in the educational community there is no consensus about the overarching purpose (singular) of schooling. We hear about this and that purpose, but all of them *in practice* rest not on a conception of the teacher as a performing artist but as a kind of civil drill sergeant required to enforce educational standards, the relationship of which to productive thinking and learning has not been demonstrable. And there are more than a few teachers who in the quiet of the night or in private conversation will say just that. Let it be noted that in regard to preparatory programs, studies have demonstrated that teachers judge their adequacy in negative terms.

Organizing this book had its problems. Initially I sought to identify and describe major aspects of performers and the performing arts and then compare those aspects to their presence and manifestation in the thinking and actions of the performing teacher. Writing about the one and then the other was like describing a Ping-Pong match. Besides, it quickly became apparent that if I pursued that course the reader would get far from an adequate picture of the development either of the performing artist or the teacher as performer. Writers are not performing artists, but they do have at least one aspect in common: each seeks to make his or her story believable. When I say *believe* I mean the audience recognizes and accepts the story.

I decided that the initial chapters should be devoted to certain features of the performing artist: how and why the career was chosen, how one is prepared for such a career, wherein the artistry inheres, the psychological aspects of role taking, external influences on performance, the obligations and relationship to the audience, and the social-institutional context in which the artist works. These are discussed in far from exhaustive detail, but sufficiently, I hope, to allow the reader to follow my argument. Following those initial chapters, I then look at teachers, schools, and preparatory programs in terms of the same features I previously discussed. The contrasts are not favorable to educators. It could be argued that there is no inherent virtue in looking at teaching from a new vantage point, especially one that on the surface appears so unrelated to teachers in schools. I quite agree. But as I have discussed elsewhere (Sarason, 1996b), it has long been claimed that schools and school systems are unique *organizations* not at all comparable to business organizations. It is one thing to say schools are different organizations and quite another thing to say they are unique. As organizations schools are different but not unique; they do share important commonalities which, when recognized, illuminate what they are or are not and what they should be. Similarly, an orchestra conductor or dancer or singer seems worlds apart from a teacher in a classroom. This book is an attempt to demonstrate that despite obvious differences they are kissing cousins. Our tendency to pin different labels on different people has both positive and negative consequences. For example, it is a glimpse of the obvious to say that a woman who is a secretary or an executive or an airplane pilot is in the category labeled "worker." But we do not call her a worker if she stays home, manages the myriads of affairs a house-home requires, rears children, etc. A moment's reflection tells us that the woman at home is working, that what she does is literally not unique; she does different things in a very different "non-work" setting but does that mean that how she thinks and plans, how she approaches and solves problems, how she handles a variety of people in and around her home, how her conception of her role changes with time, how she and others judge how well she discharges her obligation—how all of this and more has nothing important in common with those we conventionally label as workers? Labels help us see differences, and that is an important function, but labels also prevent us from seeing commonalities which have practical import.

Since World War II, and as never before in our national history, the adequacy of our schools has been center stage. Why this is so is far beyond the purposes of this book. It is also beyond my knowledge and power truly to comprehend and integrate the many facets of the question. I have written about certain aspects (e.g., Sarason, 1990b, 1993a, 1993b, 1995, 1996b) which, obviously, I considered important in some ultimate way. But there is one aspect I have always considered of bedrock importance because if this aspect continues to be dealt with in the ways that it has been, the educational reform movement will go nowhere. And that conclusion, which I arrived at in 1987 (Sarason, Davidson, & Blatt) has recently been substantiated by the report of the *National Commission on Teaching and America's Future* (1996) for which Professor Linda Darling-Hammond was executive director. My conclusion has been that unless we change and improve the selection and training of educators the fruits of educational reform efforts will be minimally edible. There will have to be other changes, to be sure, but that one is crucial.

I did not write this book to reiterate that conclusion, and I certainly did not write it to criticize teachers because, as I have written umpteen times before, to criticize teachers is to blame the victim. I wrote it because I think I have something new to say. What I have to say is in no inconsiderable way based on what teachers and students have told me over the decades, and has forced me time and again to mull over my suggestions for change and to seek and to be open to new ones. As an author I know that it is the reader who will judge the value of this book.

CHAPTER 2

Performing Artists and Audiences

In conventional usage performing artists are those who present themselves to an audience for any or all of several purposes: to stimulate, instruct, please, or entertain. When we watch or hear a performing artist, we make certain assumptions, most of which we take for granted and do not articulate. The first is that the artist wants to perform, it is not an involuntary act; the artist is there to achieve purposes not the least of which is to receive acceptance and applause, the acid test of which is that the audience leaves disposed to watch or hear the artist on another occasion. The second is that the performing artist has rehearsed for the occasion; i.e., we take for granted that the artist has spent thought, time, and energy preparing for the performance, just as we assume that *this* performance is but the latest in a long series of performances which, so to speak, established the artist's "credentials" to present him or herself on the occasion we are watching or hearing. The third assumption is that the artist will give his or her "all" to the performance and will not leave us with the impression that he or she has gone through the motions, relatively devoid of personal feeling or involvement. We may end up not liking the performance for a variety of reasons, but we truly feel cheated if we conclude that the artist was not putting out effort; treating the occasion in an uninspired, superficial way.

The fourth assumption is more subtle and complex: The artist has adopted a role the requirement of which is to instill in the audience thoughts and feelings which temporarily blur or even erase the distinction between the artist as performer and the artist as a person. We in the audience want to believe—we assume we will believe—that our reactions are also those of the artist. So, for example, when as a concert soloist Luciano Pavarotti finishes a song, he noticeably tilts his head back, closes his eyes, as if to say, "I have been in the grips of the feelings and emotions consistent with the content of the song's words and music, and I need time to get over what I experienced, to shift from Pavarotti the performer to Pavarotti the person." When he began the song or aria, it was his hope that the audience would "lose itself" the way he would, i.e., we would temporarily be different than our accustomed selves, we would be "moved," we would be taken "out of ourselves" during an interval having all of the features of *an experience* so well described by John Dewey in his *Art as Experience* (1934).

When the performance is over we make a positive or negative judgment or, not infrequently, we are ambivalent, indecisive. Was it worth it? Were we stimulated? Instructed? Entertained? Are we glad it is over? Rather than saying we make a judgment, it is more correct to say we have a judgment, i.e., a spontaneous, unreflective reaction. We may mull over that reaction and then make or not make another judgment. Generally speaking, members of an audience do not go much beyond judgments of liking or disliking. That is less true for the performer who may hear the loud and sustained audience applause but who knows or believes that his or her performance was wanting in certain important ways; it was far from a flawless performance. The judgments of performers and audiences are not perfectly correlated. Performers may regard their performance as near flawless and be puzzled by an obviously unimpressed, unresponsive audience. Performers are used to saying that they can tell when the right kind of chemistry exists between them and the audience: no whispering, no coughing, no leaving of seats, no one dozing, just rapt attention and silence, and at the end obvious, prolonged, sincere applause. Performers want to be oblivious of the audience; they do not want to be reminded that the audience in subtle or unsubtle ways is not taking kindly to the performance. A dissatisfied audience is a performer's bad dream; the wish behind the dream got derailed.

It is a glimpse of the obvious to say that the performer assumes that the audience has taken on the obligation to see, hear, feel, and respond, which is another way of saying that the audience will be respectful of the performer's intentions to provide it a satisfying experience. The performer knows that members of the audience have different reasons for coming, but, nevertheless, they have assumed the obligation to be sincerely respectful and attentive. What is less obvious is that the audience assumes that the performer has felt obliged to adapt the style and content of the performance to certain features and characteristics of the audience. That is to say, just as most members of an audience know something about the performers (individually or as a group), the performers know something about the audience: the likely age range, social class, minimum educational level, and artistic taste as each varies with city, cost of tickets, subscription lists, or sponsoring organization, as well as what the artist has learned from others who have performed before that type of audience. The performer has an idea, however vague it may be, about "where that audience is or is coming from." There are few if any performers who have not misjudged the type of this or that audience. Performers try to adapt to those features or characteristics, although they vary in the degree to which they adapt. Probably more than any other type of performer, the comedian adapts to the ways in which audiences vary in the characteristics I have mentioned. It used to be that comedians would make sport of different ethnic, racial, and religious groups, but they now studiously avoid anything that might offend those groups. And that also happened in films.

A distinction is made between "commercial" and "experimental" (or artistic avant-garde) film and theater. And one of those distinctions, a major one, concerns the question: What do audiences want and expect? The commercial production seeks to satisfy those wants and expectations; the non-commercial seeks to instruct, to alter the accustomed expectations of audiences. The commercial film, theater, and television industries spend a lot of time and money finding out what different age groups say they want to see in order to satisfy the expectations of those groups. That clearly is not the intent—if only because they lack the money—of those in the non-commercial arena; they know that at best they may attract a small, highly self-selected audience which will spread the word.

I have been emphasizing the expectations of performers and audiences because they play a crucial role in determining judgments and why they change over time, if and when they do. That is especially true when a new work of art is being performed for the first time. As an example I shall discuss the world premiere of *Porgy and Bess* by the Gershwins and DuBose (Alpert, 1990) in 1935. Long before the opening it was public knowledge that George Gershwin had been composing music for a production based on the book by Heyward (1925) and that it would be a marked departure from anything he had done before. Would it be a variant of a Broadway musical or something more operatic? Would a production with an all black cast, centering on a slice of black culture of a particular time and place in Charleston, South Carolina, be well received? If those questions were being asked by a curious general public, musical community, and musical critics, they were also being asked by the performers who knew that a great deal was at stake for them as individuals as well as for American musical tradition, history, and culture. They had, of course, great hopes and expectations, but they also knew that the realities of American society in no way ensured that audiences would receive them and the production with the dispassion and respect with which they ordinarily accord a musical work of art. That they were prepared to give their all goes without saying. And it also goes without saying that they hoped that their artistry would engender in the audience the thoughts, feelings, and emotions they as performers were depicting even though the cultural, racial, and interpersonal dynamics being depicted would be foreign to almost everyone in that audience. Would they as performers be believable? Would the music be judged positively but their artistry not? Or would both be negatively judged? They knew two things. First, precisely because the premiere performance was in New York City, it was not unrealistic to expect that many in the audience would not be "turned off" by the contents of *Porgy and Bess*. If they did not underestimate audience receptivity, neither did they overestimate it; it was an open question. Second, George Gershwin was an acclaimed and much beloved icon in American popular music and the Broadway musical theater. Granted that Gershwin was best known for his popular songs, he had composed "serious" music which people loved and flocked to hear (Concerto in F, *American in Paris*, *Cuban Overture*, *Rhapsody in Blue*, Preludes for Piano).

In the audience were music critics whose judgments would appear in newspapers and magazines ranging from popular to the professional. Their expectations were mixed but related. Was *Porgy and Bess* a musical, or an opera, or what? They well knew that standard repertoire of opera companies did not, for all practical purposes, include the works of American composers; opera meant European opera. Operas by Americans were undistinguished, and compared to European operas, they were unworthy. In the distant future the story may change, but that change was not on the horizon. Besides, on what basis could one expect that a composer of popular songs, an exemplar of American jazz and its rhythms, could even approximate the standards, quality, scope, and range of opera? The critics, especially the more "serious" ones, came with low expectations, a "show me" stance compounded of skepticism and the feeling that they would probably be witness to an overambitious effort to elevate American music, an instance of "musical climbing" akin to social climbing. They would not deny that Gershwin was a superb composer of popular songs, that he had already demonstrated a desire to venture beyond that form, but those efforts were a frail basis for expecting that what he would come up with would allow them to dignify it as opera. Classification, categorization, pigeon-holing was one of their professional tasks, and it was one that carried with it judgments of worthiness. And precisely because *Porgy and Bess* had been heralded as innovative, as a radical departure, these critics would not avoid the judgmental implication of classification.

Critics aside, what were the expectations of the audience? They expected that anything George Gershwin wrote was worth hearing and, more than that, they would find the music moving and appealing. Even though they knew that *Porgy and Bess* would not be the conventional Broadway musical to which Gershwin had mightily contributed, their respect for what he had done allowed them to expect that his new work would not be disappointing. They were curious, respectful, and eager to be responsive and appreciative. They were not concerned with classification and its implied values. Like the performers, they wanted to be moved, to have a distinctive, satisfying experience.

Expectations and judgments change over time. Today, *Porgy and Bess* is one of the most frequently produced *American* musical productions in opera houses around the world, and it is now in the repertoire of the Metropolitan Opera House. Some of the earliest critics of *Porgy and Bess* changed their minds, not because they changed their classification but rather because *Porgy and Bess* was a moving, instructive experience, a judgment the earliest audiences had made. No performers in *Porgy and Bess* worry about audience receptivity. What they worry about is whether they can do justice to their roles and engender in the audience the feelings, emotion, sympathy, and understanding that the earliest audiences experienced. An unmoved audience of *Porgy and Bess* today is a criticism of the performers.

It makes no difference to an audience how many times an artist has performed the role. They expect that person to perform as if it was the first time the artist is performing the role. Audiences do not want to feel that they are being treated to a routinized performance devoid of the appearance of spontaneity and feeling. Audiences do not want to become aware that the artist is acting; they want to identify with the role, they want to "lose themselves," to be caught up in the welter of thought and feeling the role requires. Audiences want to be respected, not to feel they are being taken for granted, as if they will not know the difference between a performer giving his or her all and one going through the motions, one who is "capturing" the audience and one who is keeping them at arm's length. All of this, of course, defines the obligation of the performer as well as pointing to the pressures the artist experiences, especially if the role is one the artist has performed scores or hundreds of times. A friend of mine saw Yul Brynner in *The King and I* when, decades ago, it had its pre-Broadway opening in New Haven. (Those were the days when the majority of plays and musicals had their tryouts in New Haven's Schubert Theater.) Over the following decades Yul Brynner must have performed in that production a thousand or more times. My friend saw him five or six times in that role, in part because he wanted his children to see it, but also because he wanted to re-experience his joy when he first saw it. How, he asked, could Yul Brynner continue to give such stirring, unforgettable performances? That is a question which has been directed to many actors who have continuously performed a role over more than one season. The answer has been:

It is not as hard as it may seem, although it certainly is not easy. For one thing, that is my obligation. The audience has come to see *me*, and they come with expectations I'm obliged to satisfy. I cannot permit myself to let them down, even if I'm not feeling well or there are things going on in my life that are difficult and upsetting. For another thing, no two audiences are the same; evening audiences are not the same as matinee audiences, just as I am not the same person today I was yesterday. When you are insensitive to audiences, when you have forgotten your obligation, it is time to quit. Finally, if before the curtain rises your heart does not start to beat faster, you don't have a queasy feeling in your stomach, your thoughts are elsewhere and not on becoming your assigned role, it is also time to quit or to re-examine yourself. Becoming another person is not easy, it is not as natural as it may seem, but when the final curtain goes down and you get the reactions of an appreciative audience, you look forward to tomorrow's performance. For me, I am as good as my last performance, and I don't always feel good.

Audiences are silent performers. They are silent but not passive, at least they did not come expecting to be inwardly passive. They come expecting to see themselves and a slice of life differently. They do not expect to be bored, unmoved, and sorry they came. They come to be transported, not to remain their accustomed selves. Audiences expect actors to *be* their roles, however different that "being" is from their everyday being. To the extent the performer can engender that illusion in the audience, the artist has discharged his or her obligation to the audience. That is why sometimes audiences are curious when an actor takes on a role radically different from one in which they are accustomed to think of him or her. That is to say, audiences have come to believe that the role reflects "real life" characteristics of the actor as a person. Let me give a personal example.

In the nineteen thirties and forties Luigi Antonelli always played in movies the role of the evil, murderous, Mafia-type gangster. His name and physical appearance (plus his artistry, of course) contributed to audiences seeing him as not only in a thoroughly despicable role but also as a not-very-likable person. That is to say, anyone who could perform so well in such a villainous role was not a person you would want to be with on a deserted island; what he exhibited in the role was saying something about him as a person. Not long after World War II I read in the paper that Luigi Antonelli would be in the starring role in a stage production of Morris West's *The Devil's Advocate*. That role is about an English Catholic, a monsignor who had worked for years in the Vatican in the service of a cardinal. He is an introverted, constricted, sincerely and devotedly religious person for whom interpersonal intimacy has been a rare occurrence. He finds out that he has terminal cancer and will die within the year. The cardinal, a fatherly, psychologically astute figure, understands the monsignor's plight and asks him to take on the task of conducting an inquiry to determine whether or not there are grounds for considering sanctification, which has been proposed by a bishop in a rural parish for a man in whose name and spirit miracles have been claimed. It is a type of inquiry requiring belief and disbelief, sympathy and detachment, interpersonal sensitivity and restrained personal expressiveness. He is given the task because, the cardinal says, he will come to know himself better, be more understanding of himself and others, be better able to accept his mortality, and perform a valuable service to his church.

I had read the novel. It is one of my all-time favorites. What stupid director thought that Luigi Antonelli could do justice to that multi-layered role? This I had to see! Luigi Antonelli—no guns, no leering, no brutality, in a role about love, human frailty, devotion, and passion in its many forms. It was one of the peak experiences I have ever had in the theater. I was initially skeptical, then flabbergasted, and then enthralled. I would be happy if I found myself on a desert island with Luigi Antonelli!

Audiences come with diverse expectations, but among them the most important is that the performer will "get" them "out of themselves," will transport them willingly and unreflectively into another world. When that audience is bored, unbelieving, and their thoughts, feelings, and fantasies are unrelated to the performance, we say the performer has "lost" the audience. Some performers will blame the audience; that is to say, they do not believe they lost the audience but rather that the audience lacked receptivity, understanding, and the proper kind and degree of motivation. Performers, like everyone else (including the audience), have difficulty directing blame to themselves.

Relatively speaking, it is infrequent that an entire performance involves only one artist. For example, a comedian like Jackie Mason is alone on the stage throughout the performance. Julie Harris as Emily Dickinson, Christopher Plummer as John Barrymore, Gary Sinese as Harry Truman literally gave solo performances. And so do concert pianists: They and the piano are the only occupants of the stage. It is far more frequent that the performances involve more, sometimes much more, than one performer, even though the focus of the audience is only a few of them. And, it needs to be emphasized, what we call a performance is not understandable apart from a variety of people we never see but who nevertheless are crucial to what we see. They perform "behind" the scenes. In the next chapter I shall explore some of the implications of (1) the nature, quality, and structure of the relationships among the performers whom we do see and (2) those same factors in regard to the relationships between the performers and those we do not see. A performance is a highly *organized* end product of a complicated process and *organization*. The artist is not a law unto him- or herself. For good or for bad, the organization, seen or unseen, affects the performance.

CHAPTER 3

Performers and the Organizational Context

When we attend the performance of a symphony orchestra, we may say we are part of the audience; the performers are on stage. From the standpoint of the diverse kinds of players who make up that orchestra, who is their audience? Phenomenologically, the players have two audiences: the conventionally defined and placed audience and the conductor. They are playing for the conductor, by which we mean that they seek to perform in accord with his interpretation of the score: how and when each section should play, sound, and integrate with other sections. During rehearsals and the live performance the players know that the conductor is concerned with more than technical proficiency but also with the feeling tone the player should convey. When we say a person is a professor, we mean that he or she has something to profess: he or she has a point of view, a distinctive way of organizing and giving life to the dry facts of the subject matter. Two professors teaching the same course to similar students will differ in small or large ways in regard to how they organize the subject matter, and present it to (perform for) and involve their audience of students. In one case the students may employ a musical simile to describe the professor: He or she is a "prima donna" who has one and only one point of view and brooks no challenge to it. In the other case the students may feel they can engage in a give-and-take with the professor with safety and productive clarification even though they know that on their performance in the final examination they must be able to demonstrate at the very least that they understand the professor's point of view.

Conductors are professors, a fact that is obvious to veterans of a symphony orchestra. Over the years these veterans have played for several conductors each of whom was distinctive as a person and as a conductor, requiring them to unlearn and learn this or that way of interpreting and playing. Sometimes they find the process of adaptation productive and enlivening; other times they find it irritating, dispiriting, demeaning. The social psychological context may produce reactions varying from smooth to explosive, from relief to a mutinous sullenness. As in any organization where leadership changes, the substance of the rumor and gossip mill changes. It is a mill with many leaks, especially when the players are unhappy with the conductor. In subtle and unsubtle ways some players convey messages to board members and other higher-ups in the organization, and those messages are also conveyed to music critics. And given the fact that the players belong to a union, their diverse reactions can be conveyed via that "communication network."

No conductor seeks to lose or alienate his or her audience of players. He or she wants to shape or mold the diversity of players so as to produce his or her kind of sound and total effect. Some succeed and some do not. When they do not, they direct blame to the orchestra: their recalcitrance, their lack of musicianship, their rigidity. That kind of blame assignment is not directed to all players; some players or sections are blamed more than others, a fact that can increase the force associated with another fact: When you have 40 or more musicians in an orchestra, you have different personalities, rivalries, and judgments of competence and excellence.

It is not unusual that a significant number of the musicians do not like a conductor but respect him for the breadth of his knowledge, musical standpoint, his "ear," devotion to the score, and his high standards. They may see him as a tyrannical taskmaster, as prone to explosive outbursts of dissatisfaction, or too aloof and too impressed with himself. But if they have respect for his musicianship, if they have concluded that warts and all, he is concerned only with doing justice to the composer's intent and not with elevating his self-esteem, if they have come to feel that he respects their musicianship, they separate, so to speak, his personal qualities from what he is as a conductor. It is, of course, quite another story when they do not respect him as a conductor.

The audience does not come to the symphony concert hall to judge the total organization. They come to hear the music. More often than not, most of the program contains music they have heard before. They come to re-experience what had previously given them significant personal satisfaction, usually with another conductor and orchestra. If this performance compares unfavorably with the previous one, they will tend to blame the conductor more than the players. That the explanation may be more complicated is not something they consider, unless on subsequent occasions with that same conductor and orchestra they continue to find themselves making unfavorable comparisons. When they learn that a new conductor has been chosen, they are relieved, not surprised, but even so they do not see the decision as reflective of the dynamics of a complicated organization. The point here is that the performance we hear is never independent of that total organization. The effect of that organization may be minimal, but it is never nonexistent. When we say that this conductor and orchestra are consistently superb, we are also praising (usually unknowingly) those parts of the organization we never see. When a conductor and orchestra give us pedestrian, uninspiring performances, it again says a good deal about the parts of the organization we never see. If audiences are unaware of those parts, the conductor and the players are; they know that what we see and hear on the stage is affected by those unseen parts. Anyone who is knowledgeable about the economics of symphonic organizations needs no convincing on that score.

Let us turn now to a consideration of audience. When he or she is conducting, back to the audience, the conductor's audience is the orchestra, just as he or she is the orchestra's audience. Yes, both know there is an audience "out there," but in their role as conductor or players they serve as audiences for each other. If queried they will say they perform to serve the audience in the hall, but while they are performing they are minimally, if at all, aware of that audience. They are a mutually dependent, interacting group, and from the standpoint of the audience it is the conductor who gets their attention; the players are playing, the conductor is performing.

In the theater there is no conductor between the actors and the audience. At different times and in different degrees and ways, each actor on the stage gets the attention of the audience. The performer may be in a bit or a more major role, but he or she gets noticed by the audience. In the theater the audience sees, hears, and responds to the actors with a concreteness or singularity unlike how they experience the players in an orchestra where, for example, they do not see, hear, and respond to players in the violin section as singular performers. In the concert hall we hear and experience *music*; in the theater we experience *people, individuals*, each of whom is literally in a unique role. And regardless of the size of the role, we expect the performer to be believable, not for us to call into question their artistry, but to "fit in" with the ongoing action to further it in some way. We come expecting to be witness to a story having different roles and that each actor in his or her assigned role will contribute to our understanding of that role in relation to the others in the play. The believability of a performer in a role is one thing; believability in regard to the relationship of that performer to performers in other roles is another thing. A symphony is about the relationships of sounds; a play is about the relationships of people. A role in a play always takes its meaning in relation to other roles. We expect the performers to make that relation understandable, and convincing. It is as if we say to the performers, "We know that each role is different. Convince us that they go together. We know that each of you is in a distinctive role. Show us how that distinctiveness contributes to a distinctively convincing total effect."

The reaction of an audience to a play may range from the totally negative to an unalloyed positive one. Whether it is on the negative or positive side of the continuum, we pass judgment on the actors or the playwright, or both. Although we know in the abstract that the play had a producer, financial backers, and a director, our judgment is not directed to and does not include them. The history of the theater has more than its share of productions marked by internecine warfare between them (the unseen) and the performers (the seen). And some of the battles between performers have attained legendary status. In the book *The Playmakers* (1970) Little and Cantor describe the diverse aspects of a production:

> Actors work with each other and their collaborators in the theater according to very specific, largely unwritten, and universally recognized commandments. If one were to codify the major actors' commandments they might read something like this: Thou shalt not "upstage" a fellow actor; nor interrupt his speeches; nor move conspicuously on his lines; nor ruin another actor's laugh by any means, motivated or otherwise; honor the playwright and read the lines as they are written.
>
> Such rules are elementary, recognized by all actors. And they are broken all the time. Since an actor is instinctively tempted to think a play is about him and that his role is the key part, he frequently "improves" on his lines. As an actress acknowledges, "This abuses the material, abuses the other actors, abuses the directorial concept." The older playwrights find improvisation intolerable and "Method" actors the worst offenders; Paddy Chayefsky doesn't appreciate spontaneous line-readings by actors. He says, "I really wouldn't mind, if only most actors didn't improvise such lousy lines."
>
> It is the director's job to hold the actors not only to the words but to the theme of the play, and not allow them to go wandering off into quixotic self-expression. A good director must resolve the conflict between his higher allegiance to the overall concept and the actor's fierce drive to interpret the play in terms of his own part. (pp. 106–107)

Shumlin finds that a special atmosphere obtains when rehearsals commence. All is euphoric, the cast and collaborators are alight with optimism. There is a great coming together with single purpose, says Shumlin: "Everyone involved throws himself into the pot: flesh, bones, color of hair disappear . . . It is a remarkable thing that takes place. It happens right away, and in my experience it always happens. People are not conscious of it at all. I recognize it, because as the director I have already shaped the play in my own mind. Maybe something will be a little wrong—something about the play, an actor in his part. But spiritually the thing will still happen. Each will have cast himself into the forge in which the metal, the amalgam, will be made, as they are modified by the play and as they themselves modify the play."

As rehearsals continue, euphoria dissolves and a change comes over the members of the cast. Shumlin notices that the actors begin to rely on their own judgments. They begin to question, to criticize, to analyze, as they grow more confident of their own abilities. At this stage, by thinking of himself at the expense of the group, an actor can be destructive. "Now," Shumlin says, "the director must hold a firm hand over the cast. He can be rewarded by the creativity that comes out of the actor exploring his own way, but he must find a tolerable level of permissiveness. You very quickly recognize when an actor has more to offer than you originally expected of him."

In the last days of rehearsal, the great coming together of the early days must repeat itself. The end meets the purpose of the beginning as the deadline approaches. "This factor creates its own dynamic," says Shumlin. "Time is rapidly diminishing. And this works to re-create the spirit that existed on the first day." The cycle is complete, and a show is born. (pp. 156–157)

A most hilarious and detailed account of conflict in a production concerns George Bernard Shaw's production of *Pygmalion* (Huggett, 1969). Shaw was the playwright, producer, and director. There was never any doubt in Shaw's mind about how the play should be staged and acted. In fact, the world premiere of *Pygmalion* was in a foreign country, and its English production was delayed several years because Shaw did not think it could be appropriately staged, acted, and appreciated in England. To say that Shaw knew what he wanted is to understate the truth. How he wooed Mrs. Patrick Campbell for the role of Eliza Doolittle! Mrs. Campbell very much wanted the role but refused to come to terms unless she could choose *her* Higgins. She wanted no part of Robert Loraine, who was Shaw's choice. The imp in Shaw knew how to woo Mrs. Campbell:

I don't want anything put before me. I am an artist and don't understand finance. I want my Liza and I want my Higgins. If you are unkind about them I shall sit down and cry until I get them. I won't choose between them. I must have my Liza and no other Liza. There is no other Liza and there can be no other Liza. I wrote the play to have my Liza. And I must have a proper Higgins for my Liza. I won't listen to reason: I will sit there and howl. I can howl for twenty years, getting louder and louder all the time . . . I won't be offered the Best and then refused poor Bobby, who is the best. I will have a better if you can find him, because nobody is good enough for my Liza . . . I don't want to force anybody into anything. I only want to see my play with my Liza properly supported in it; and until I get that I want to do nothing but yell . . .

I have gone through my card index and could name you twenty far better Higginses than any you have thought of; but they are none of them good enough; I'd rather die than see you dragged down to second class by them: I'd as soon ask you to wear a contract dress at £3.4s.2d. If you won't have Loraine then we must wait until somebody else whom you will have comes to the front and proves his mettle. And I shall cry, cry, cry all the time, and there will be a great wave of public feeling against you for your cruelty. And I will write such a play for Lena Ashwell, my dear Lena who really loves me. So there! (pp. 34–35)

Finally, though, Shaw gave up on Loraine and settled on Sir Beerbohm Tree for the role of Professor Higgins. Choosing and wooing Sir Tree were done more subtly and with consummate skill by Shaw.

Shaw, neither publicly nor privately, viewed himself as selfless, as no more than a vehicle for enhancing the glory and accomplishments of two stars. What Shaw did not bargain for was that that was precisely the way Mrs. Campbell and Sir Tree viewed Shaw. He had made them feel absolutely crucial; they were doing him a favor. War took place up until opening night. Huggett states that if Shaw had known what he was getting into by having two stars who viewed a leader like Shaw as someone who would benefit from their radiance, he would not have gone ahead. This conclusion seems more true for the two stars than for Shaw who, realist that he was, knew what he was up against and would have to do. Indeed, Huggett seems unaware that he describes Shaw as relishing the whole affair. Shaw knew more about what was going to happen than either of his stars. He judged them far better than they did him. Shaw felt he could pull it off, namely, that he could stage a performance that would meet his standards as well as meet the needs of his stars. He was temporarily successful. When Shaw left for vacation after the opening, Mrs. Campbell and Sir Tree slowly but steadily changed the production according to their styles. What he had won by virtue of his authority and authoritarianism was lost in his absence.

When we see a play we do not see a conductor, but we know that what we see had and has the equivalent: the director. The performers we see on the stage very much reflect his or her imprint. However much those performers may wish it otherwise, they are not at liberty to do whatever they like; in large and small ways they have to go along with the director's viewpoints. That is why it is not infrequent that there are changes in the cast before the play opens. From the standpoint of the director, a performer is someone to be molded to conform to his or her interpretations of roles. From the standpoint of the performer, conformity comes with a price which may be small or large, small in the sense of being tolerable or so large as to be intolerable or dispiriting or disillusioning or all of these. If when we see a play we do not see a director, it is not because the director has left the production as if his or her task is finished. Directors (like Shaw) may go on vacation or take on another production, but from time to time they come back to cast a critical eye. And, as in the case of Shaw, they may not like what they see. That assumes, of course, that the play did not close shortly after it opened! In that case everyone, those we see and those we do not, conducts his or her own autopsy on why the patient died and who bears major responsibility. Opinions will vary about who committed professional malpractice. When a play has been critically acclaimed and has run for months, a critical point frequently occurs when one of the major performers leaves the cast and a new performer "takes over." That point is critical because *no one* in the organization, let alone the remaining performers, wants the new performer to "take over" in the sense of transforming the production except in small idiosyncratic ways. "If it ain't broke, don't fix it" is the stance of everyone. The transition may be uneventful, it may also be a festering source of conflict causing other performers to leave the cast.

The point I have been making is conceptually obvious but visually it is not: The production we see is not understandable only in terms of what we see. We see performers, we do not see the organization in which the performers have been and are embedded. Performers know that, audiences do not. We come to the theater to see and judge performers in a play, not to become aware of producers, financial backers, directors, stage designers, and even the playwright. We come willingly to become engaged by the realities depicted on the stage, not by the realities of the producing organization. We come to "lose ourselves," not to be reminded of what we experience daily in our work in organizations. Except, of course, if that is the point of the play, and even then we are not aware that the point applies to the organization producing the play.

There is another way of making the point that will be familiar to many readers. Over the decades I have taken the opportunity to see theatrical productions more than one time, on each occasion by a different company. If no two people are the same, neither are two productions of the same play. We expect there will be differences, but we do not expect differences so striking that we are truly surprised, positively or negatively. We may see the play in a new light: as more nuanced, more believable, more compelling, more thought provoking. Or we may see it as labored, lacking spark, pedestrian. Either way, we are most likely to attribute the differences we experienced to features of the performers. That explanation, of course, may have merit but less merit than in instances where the performers we witnessed had comparable experience and celebrity. Our explanation is not likely to praise or criticize producers or directors (or both), as if what we saw on the two occasions is explainable *only* in terms of the performers. This point has been made by Edith Hamilton in regard to the translations of the plays of the dramatists in ancient Greece. The works of these dramatists have been translated and retranslated scores of times. Many of those translations leave us cold, and we wonder why these dramas are held in such reverential esteem. We blame the "overrated" dramatist, not a poor translation. Hamilton then proceeds to present her translation, side by side with others, and the sun comes out, the clouds disappear, and the artistry and brilliance of the play comes gloriously to the fore. You change your mind about the Greek dramatists. At least, that was my experience. The stage director is like a translator whom we do not see. The director is given acknowledgment in the program, the translator is acknowledged in small type on the title page of the book. When we read the play, we do not think about the translator; when we see a play, we do not think about the director. In the former we experience the written word, in the latter our eyes are on the performers.

Nothing I have said in this chapter was intended in any way to deny the crucial role of the artistry of the performer in what we see, experience, and judge. One of the definitions my dictionary gives for an artist is "One who professes and practices an art in which conception and execution are governed by taste and imagination." An architect is an artist; the builder who constructs the house from the blueprints is an artisan. Both may exercise taste and imagination, but the difference in degree in such an exercise is a difference that makes a difference. The point of this chapter is that the kind of performing artist I have discussed is always operating under constraints (organizational constraints) from others we never do see. If audiences do not know or are not aware of that, performers certainly do know it. The clearest examples I know are accounts by some of George Balanchine's most acclaimed ballerinas. We in the audience never saw Balanchine; we would have been surprised to learn that for these ballerinas the audience was Balanchine. The unseen is always a factor in a performance. That factor may be positive or negative, large or small. It is never zero.

How does one become a performer in the arts? Who chooses them? By what criteria? What determines longevity in a performing career and changes, up or down, in quality of performance? Let us in the next chapter turn to these questions.

CHAPTER 4

The Nurturing of Interest and Talent

It is generally the case in the performing arts that interest in and desire to become an artist starts at an early age, usually before adolescence. In the case of dance and music (violin, piano), for example, a performing career is very problematic if the individual's interest and desire begin after he or she has entered the teen years. Although interest and desire are features of an individual, their sources and strengths are not. A particular performance to which they were taken, parental influence, movies, TV, and even books may play crucial roles in stimulating and reinforcing interest and desire. The presence of a piano in the home can be and has been decisive for a young child. In any event, interest and desire very much depend on social-familial contexts which can be pressuring, or supportive, or insensitive to the young person's interest and desire. In supporting the child's interest and desire, neither parents nor child may have the expectation that it may lead to a performing career. Indeed, parents may view such a career very negatively. The crucial point is when on their own parents conclude, or the child's teacher concludes, that the child has unusual talent which should be nurtured. The parents find themselves asking several questions. How do we find out if our child has unusual talent? How do we nurture that talent? What future steps may be necessary to exploit that talent? What are we letting ourselves and our child in for? Parents may not know very much about a performing career, but one thing most of them know: At different times in different places and with different people their child will receive instruction. Interest, desire, and talent are necessary but not sufficient for becoming a performing artist. Instruction, continuous instruction, is necessary. How do you get to Carnegie Hall? And the answer is practice, practice, practice. The answer is, of course, humorous but incomplete because it leaves out the teachers whose criticisms, interpretive suggestions, and direction require a good deal of practice. Talent without instruction is raw talent. It may allow you to become an usher at Carnegie Hall, but you will never be onstage.

We are used to hearing physicians say what a long arduous path they have to traverse to become licensed as a physician; to traverse that path takes years of instruction from numerous teachers. Performing artists can justifiably say the same thing except that their path began well before college and involved hours of daily practice with diverse teachers. If there is anything common to the life histories of performing artists it is that interest, desire, and talent were present and recognized early in their lives. They defined what their lives were and would become, even though, unlike physicians, they could not be assured recognition and even a liveable income. It is as if a performing career was experienced as "a calling," a willing submission to the call of destiny and fate.

Let me now relate two types of personal experience. I am a fellow of Silliman College, one of Yale's living quarters for undergraduates. Dr. Kelly Brownell is the Silliman master and a colleague I came to know when he accepted a position in the department of psychology. He is himself a musician of the country blues genre. When he became master, he instituted a series of Sunday musical brunches at which Silliman students perform as pianists, violinists or cellists, or singers. The music is classical. Given their age, after the first concert I regarded their artistry and stage presence as only a shade less than amazing. That judgment did not change after the remaining concerts at each of which there were different students. They were musicians long before they came to Yale, and they had taken advantage of any opportunity to perform. A decisive factor in their choosing Yale was its school of music where they not only could receive instruction from different members of the faculty but would also be provided with opportunity to perform and to see and hear leading established performers. Not all the student performers sought performing careers, but among them were some who would have dearly sought such a career if they felt more positively about the dimensions of their talent. I was struck by the readiness with which they acknowledged that in some ultimate sense interest and desire were necessary but not sufficient bases for making final career decisions. Most of the student performers were seeking performing careers but here again they acknowledged that the road ahead would not be smooth and would be demanding of a total personal and professional commitment in a sphere of activity in which there would be many talented—some extraordinarily talented—individuals competing for recognition. They knew what they were letting themselves in for, and they would give it their best shot. Listening to these students I was reminded of studies I had done years before on career choices of graduating seniors who chose medicine as a career (Sarason, 1977). Suffice it to say here that these students had remarkably unrealistic expectations of what a medical career entailed in terms of personal freedom and growth, the economics of medicine, and the pluses and minuses of narrow specialization, and in a profession that at the time was beginning to undergo dramatic changes. Compared to these would-be physicians, the student musical performers were paragons of a realistic perspective, paragons enough for some to be dissuaded from a performing career. As one student (Japanese) said to me, "I would like to be a Yo-Yo Ma; I'll try, but the odds are not in my favor."

The second personal experience concerns children of several friends who sought careers in the theater. Unlike those who seek careers in other performing arts, the decision to seek a career in the theater, or even to contemplate one, does not (except rarely) take place in early childhood but rather in the mid teen years. Before those years the fantasy of becoming an actor may have been there: they may be seen as good "imitators," as having no qualms whatsoever of "performing" before others, as indeed relishing the appreciation that family and friends do articulate. But it is not until they participate in a theatrical production and fantasy receives support from experience that a career in the theater begins to be considered. What may follow? Let me illustrate by the son, Joshua Weinstein, of my friends Rhona and Harvey Weinstein. By the time Joshua was graduated from high school he had participated in numerous productions, leaving him and others with no doubt that he was talented. He chose a college where he could expect his interest, desire, and talent would be challenged, judged, and developed. At the same time he was a self-confident, outgoing (even brash some might say), determined young man, he knew the road ahead would not be easy. His parents were supportive but yet uneasy because they knew that attaining the status of a *professional* actor required step-by-step experiences, instruction, luck, and a degree of determination without which thousands of careers in the theater had been early aborted. To be "credentialed" as an actor, they knew, was not for the faint hearted, with or without talent. The starving or unemployed actor who drove taxicabs or waited on tables was familiar to them as it is to all of us. I admired Joshua's parents' supportive stance but could not refrain from time to time saying, "With your support, his determination and talent, luck, and food stamps, he stands a good chance." By the time he was graduated from college his theatrical experience on and off campus was considerable. In his senior year the actress Meryl Streep conducted a class at the college. Joshua met and spoke briefly with her and his parting words to her were, "Someday I will be acting with you." Immediately after graduation he had a 2-month fellowship with England's acclaimed National Shakespeare Company, where he was more onlooker and stagehand than he was actor, although he did appear in a nonspeaking role in *Midsummer Night's Dream*.

His parents visited him and observed one of the classes given by the director. Rhona (a psychologist) and Harvey (a psychiatrist) were amazed and gripped by the way the director sought to help the students experience how a particular line in a particular Shakespeare play evoked different feelings both in the students and onlookers when that line was uttered in different interpersonal contexts. Acting, Rhona and Harvey knew, was more than reciting lines, but by the end of the class they had a better appreciation of what "more" implied. Following that experience Joshua went to live in New York where he made the daily rounds in search of a part, any part, in a production. He was disappointed but not surprised that nothing was on the horizon for him. He applied and auditioned for a one year fellowship with the National Shakespeare Company in Washington. He was accepted and is there as I write these words. He knows he is a learner, he knows he has a lot more to experience, learn, and develop as an actor. He already has some credentials as an actor, and when he says that, his emphasis is on the word some.

I could tell a similar story about Scott Zigler, the son of Bernice and Edward Zigler, who is a much acclaimed colleague of mine in Yale's department of psychology. Scott early on knew that he had aunts, uncles, and cousins who had been performers in the Kansas City area. His mother said that it was in the fifth grade that he first expressed an interest in acting and that it was in high school that he acted and directed. For college he selected New York University because of its school for the performing arts. (And it was New York!) It was there that he took a class with playwright and director, David Mamet, who obviously took to him, beginning a student-teacher relationship which became one of friendship. He worked with Mamet for more than 10 years, an apprenticeship which led to the position of director of a company in Louisville. I am writing these words on October 4, 1997, a month before this 34-year-old man will "debut" as director of a new Broadway play. In signing the contract to direct the play Scott had the producer insert a clause certifying that there would be two tickets for choice seats for his parents on opening night. My guess is that 23-year-old Joshua will consider himself blessed if at 34 he will have his first major role in a recognized theater.

We are used to hearing that every male actor would like some day to have the opportunity to meet the challenge of playing Hamlet. That quip reflects the fact that performers generally seek opportunities to perform in new roles that will broaden their experience, that will test their ability and demonstrate to others new facets of their expressive artistry. Whether actor, musician (instrumental or vocal), or dancer, the performer seeks new challenging experiences. No performer willingly wants to be known as competent in only certain types of roles or with the works of a certain composer or choreographer. In each of the performing arts the performer knows there is an extensive "literature" containing challenges against which they would like to test their mettle. Performers do not like to be typecast, to be seen as having a narrow talent. But, as in the case of actors, they know that certain works and roles demand prior experiences demonstrating that they deserve the opportunity to perform them. They know they must nurture their talent and that diversity of experience is crucial. And every performer can point to instances where a colleague took on a role for which they were not prepared. From the very outset of their careers performing artists have more than inchoate ideas of the diversity of experience he or she wants and needs to be ultimately judged by self and others as more than a narrow artist. They need to experience the sense of growth, not the sense that they have no more to experience and learn. As a performer once said, "The danger point is when the artist says he has no more to experience and learn, that he is playing Beethoven or Brahms the way he did 20 years ago."

Wherein is the artistry of the performer who, so to speak, is "in between" the audience and the author (composer, choreographer, playwright)? What does a performer have to do to convey to an audience the letter *and* spirit of a work or role? We expect more from a singer than the ability to sing the right notes, just as we expect more from an actor than repeating lines from a script. Performing requires more than accuracy of memory. What the performer seeks and the audience expects is what is meant by a believable, convincing performance; the performer does not strike us as "out of character," as unconvincing, as jarring, as not "ringing true." How does the performer achieve this effect? Attempts to discuss and describe answers to that question have been most extensively given in regard to acting. It is a controversial topic but despite differences there are commonalities. For one thing, the actor has to make as serious an effort as possible to understand the role in all of its nuances, social, psychological, and interpersonal. The actor as a person is not the actor in the role; the actor has to "become" the role, however different that role is from what he or she "really" is. Saying that the actor has to identify with the role is true but unhelpful. A successful identification requires more than needing and wanting to identify. If every person is unique, so is every role, and it is capturing that uniqueness and conveying it to an audience that is the difficult obligation of the actor. By word, tone, gesture, facial expression, and "body language," the actor seeks to make the fictional character real for us.

This point has been illustrated concretely and instructively by Gurewitsch (1997) in an article entitled "Maria, Not Callas." The subtitle is "Terrence McNally's *Master Class* deliberately plays fast and loose with historical fact in search of artistic." The truth of the play about the operatic legend, Maria Callas, derived from the historical fact that the singer gave a series of 25 master classes at Juillard in 1971, as well as the fact of her failed love affair with Aristotle Onassis who then married Jackie Kennedy. Gurewitsch begins the article with two short paragraphs:

> "Art is domination. It's making people think that for that precise moment in time there is only one way, one voice. Yours."
>
> So says Maria Callas in Terrence McNally's play *Master Class*, exposing the bold hoax that none but the most exceptional practitioners are able to pull it off. When Zoe Caldwell introduced the play on Broadway, nearly two years ago, she herself perpetrated that hoax, for which she was rewarded, quite deservedly, with the fourth Tony Award of her career. Whatever one's view of the play (and lasting sentiment for and against the late diva ensured that judgments would be fierce), the role of Maria was Caldwell's property. She was a python, humorless and stern, mesmerizing in her refusal to countenance any form of compromise. Her reading was definitive, pre-emptive, exhausting all possibilities. When she departed the vehicle, it would surely fall apart.

The vehicle did not fall apart. Over the course of the next year the play continued to mesmerize audiences; Patti LuPone replaced Zoe Caldwell and then Dixie Carter replaced her. In addition to these two replacements Gurewitsch saw three other actresses: Rosella Falk in Milan, Fanny Ardant in Paris, and Faye Dunaway in the national touring company. Only Ardant "yields not an inch to Caldwell . . . LuPone runs Caldwell and Ardant a close second, with Carter a respectable third. Falk and Dunaway are nowhere in sight, yet even they have light to shed on the role's multi-faceted—though not unlimited—possibilities."

Gurewitsch makes four points. The most obvious one is that the person-role in the play is, like a "real" person, a very complicated individual. The second is that however different the quality of different actors' performances in that role may be, each in some way illuminates a different facet of the person depicted in that role. They differ, of course, in the number of facets they illuminate and how and with what force they are believably and seamlessly integrated, but each in some way illuminates one or more aspect. The third point is in the way of a hint. One of those actresses, Patti LuPone, had an experience in the recent past that *in principle* was similar to what Maria Callas had experienced with Onassis: She had, despite critical acclaim in the extensive pre-Broadway tryouts of *Sunset Boulevard*, been terminated by the producer and replaced by Glenn Close, a termination that engendered far more than a little public and legal furor. Was that experience, Gurewitsch speculates, something LuPone drew on in her understanding and depiction of the role? That speculation, of course, suggests that if we knew more about the personal lives of the other actresses

Gurewitsch saw, we could conclude what every teacher and theorist of acting proclaims: Actors should and can use personal experience to understand and identify with the role they are playing, to some extent at least, and the difference among actors inheres in how seriously and well they use themselves *and* their imagination to seek that understanding. Roles are not created out of whole and impersonal cloth.

The fourth point is not one Gurewitsch makes but it is one about him. How many people who have seen the play have the interest and opportunity to see five different actresses in the central role? That, of course, is a rhetorical question, but it serves to remind us of two things. Performers, even when they have established professional credentials, can vary considerably in the impact they have, varying from little impact to an overwhelming one. The average person (like me) in the audience of *Master Class* makes an absolute not a comparative judgment about the performance, unaware that our positive or negative judgment may change considerably with different performers. Gurewitsch tells us that after he saw Zoe Caldwell perform he could not see how anyone else could match her. What if the finest or only performance he saw was with Faye Dunaway or Rosella Falk? He tells us that there have been 40 different productions of *Master Class* in 40 foreign countries, "not to mention nine in Germany alone. Never mind the slew of productions by American regional, stock, and amateur companies, which could number in the dozens." Leaving the amateur companies aside, what if we and Gurewitsch had masochistically decided to see all of them? Would our judgments be described by a normal probability curve, or would it be skewed so that there would be a few we very highly judged and then there would be all of the rest to which we are more or less indifferent or negative? My guess is that our judgments would in no way be described by a normal probability curve. Audiences are almost always not in the position of making comparative judgments. They usually do not or cannot ask: What would our judgment be with different performers?

We took our daughter to see the road company of *My Fair Lady*. She loved it. My wife and I were, if not bored, mildly entertained even though the performers were well known and certainly competent professionals. But in the same theater in New Haven a decade before, we had seen the premiere performance starring Julie Andrews and Rex Harrison. We responded to the two performances in the same way that Gurewitsch did to the performances of Caldwell and Dunaway, although the difference between the two musicals was not as damningly large. If you have not experienced the "best," you do not know that you are settling for a noticeably lower standard.

How does or can a performer use personal experience to understand a role? That question was precisely one that Freud discussed in regard to the credentialing of psychoanalysts, and one that later became an issue in regard to anyone who sought to practice any type of psychotherapy. Freud contended that the contents and dynamics of human development not only limited and distorted self-understanding but also the comprehending of the sources and meanings of the behavior of others. Freud did not assert that people could not gain self-understanding but rather that there were clear limits to what such an effort could achieve, and that before a person takes on the responsibility of helping troubled people he or she needs more than knowledge of psychoanalytic theory and its literature. That person needs personally to experience what it means to undergo a personal psychoanalysis, to experience the *Sturm und Drang* associated with the analytic relationship, to know in the most personal, concrete, palpable way all those interpersonal forces and contexts that cause us to forget, distort, and defend against motives, fantasies, and events that were troubling, overwhelming sources of anxiety, and in one or another way and to a degree causing changes in our psychological makeup of which we are unaware. That is why he considered it absolutely necessary that a person undergo analysis before he or she seeks to understand and help others. Psychoanalytic theory, Freud emphasized, was a theory applicable not only to wouldbe analysts but to people generally; the analyst and the patient are different as personalities, but both have much in common in terms of the nature and vicissitudes of the interaction between developmental internal dynamics and external social-familial contexts. What Freud was saying to the analytic candidate was, "To the extent that you have a better understanding of how you became what you are, you have a basis for understanding how other people came to be what they are. You use your life to understand the lives of others." If there is much I can criticize in Freud's writings, it does not extend to a dictum which captures the above point: "Knowing thyself is a precondition for knowing others." There are few if any actors who would disagree, although agreement in no way means that all actors take it seriously or do it well.

What I have been saying has been most cogently, persuasively, and illuminatingly posed and discussed by Constantin Stanislavski in his book *An Actor Prepares*, which I mentioned in Chapter 1. The book was published in 1936 and my copy, purchased in 1983, indicated that it had been reprinted 37 times. It has become a kind of bible for actors. Stanislavski uses a series of examples in order to convey the developmental nature of the process of understanding a role. Understanding does not come full-blown, but rather is a result of grappling with three major obstacles: underestimating the scope and complexity of the process, failure to use one's own life experiences creatively, and resistance to the idea that the process is a never-ending one. What keeps the actor engaged in what is a demanding cognitive and affective process and quest? The answer is that the actor cares for the other person (the role) and seeks compassionately to identify with and to become the other person. That person may be hateful, unlovable, destructive, and evil, but the actor's task is to understand that person to the degree that the actor willingly and compassionately makes that person's phenomenology convincing to an audience. The actor cannot indulge his or her prejudices or values; that is, the actor cannot dislike the person. Strange to say, the actor must care for and be compassionate toward that person if the actor is to become that person. In "real life," the actor may recoil from anyone with the characteristics of an Iago, but when he seeks to play that role, he cares for Iago. You cannot "become" somebody for whom you have no feelings of caring and compassion. When one actor says that he can play Iago better than another actor, he is saying that he understands Iago better, that he is more sensitive to nuances in Iago's character and outlook, that he cares more for Iago: he has probed more deeply for the roots of Iago's thinking and behavior so that he can feel he is Iago. When an actor says he or she loves a certain role, there is a part of that actor that means it literally, however revolting that role is to the audience.

But now we come to what I consider Stanislavski's greatest insight. It is one of those insights that when articulated seems a glimpse of the obvious, but how frequently do we take the obvious seriously? The actor prepares for a particular role, and it is understandable if he or she rivets on that single role (just as the clinician rivets on the palpable person before him or her). But that role is integrally related to all other roles in the play. Can you understand a role as if it were independent of the other roles? Can you understand Iago independent of Othello or Desdemona? Is the phenomenology of one comprehensible apart from that of the others? Can the actor deal with the interdependence of roles? Concretely and ingeniously, Stanislavski illustrates why the actor should not, must not, see his or her role apart from the others. Can you understand a member of a family without seeing that person in the truly seamless psychological web of all members of the family? Long before the theoretical and practical rationale of family therapy was developed, Stanislavski had formulated the rationale and its educational-training implications. And, as was the case with family therapy, what was at stake for Stanislavski was how to improve outcomes, how this enlarged conception of the obligations of the actor would make for a more powerfully moving performance. What Stanislavski sought to inculcate in his students was an attitude of caring toward all roles in the play.

In the drama section of the *New York Times* for April 15, 1985, there was an article by Enid Nemy entitled "O'Neill Performed for Mayo Doctors." Several actors (Jason Robards, Sam Robards, Teresa Wright, Margaret Hunt) performed and read scenes from Eugene O'Neill's *Long Day's Journey into Night*. The scenes dealt with the narcotic addiction of Mary Tyrone, the wife, and the reactions of her family. The audience was 1,600 staff physicians, residents, and personnel of the Mayo Clinic and Foundation. The occasion was the fourth in an "Insight" series undertaken in 1981 to study human behavior through the medium of the theater. The director of the series explained: "We call the program 'Insight' because it is not to give answers but to give insight into the common human problems that are a great part of every physician's practice, but a small part of his or her education. Physicians don't need any more facts, and the time they can spend on human problems, their own and others, is very limited. The theater can move into that gap." One Mayo professor is quoted as saying: "We are a group of physicians who are highly subspecialized. But even for general practitioners, there is almost no formal training in subjects like alcoholism, drug addiction, aging, and suicide. Many physicians feel ill-prepared and incompetent in these areas." Another professor said: "This allows physicians to see these problems from a different aspect; we tend to see them in a more clinical way." Finally, another professor states: "One danger we have is becoming accustomed to our own methodology and not being terribly flexible in seeing things from the view of other people."

The rationale for the series requires comment. For one thing, it explicitly recognizes that physicians are deficient in their understanding of people with a chemical dependency, or who are old, or who seek to end their lives. It also recognizes that neither in their medical education nor in their practice do they have the time to gain an understanding of such "common problems." There is a third feature that I will address after discussing this question: What are the objectives of the series? I shall assume that, although the audience enjoyed the presentation, enjoyment was not a major goal. Clearly, the audience is to gain a broadened and deepened understanding of people presumably quite different from themselves, an understanding leading to and becoming intertwined with feelings of caring and compassion. Stated in this way, it is an objective to be attained not only by this audience but by any audience that sees this stirring play; that was O'Neill's objective. But this series is not meant to be simply a night in the theater watching superb actors illuminate the phenomenology of ill people. This play was presented to an audience of physicians presumably for the purpose of deepening their understanding in order to influence their subsequent actions with their patients. This, of course, raises two questions. What understanding did these medical personnel attain? How will such an understanding inform their actions? We do not and cannot know the answers to these questions. After all, the series is intended "to fill a gap," to make a difference in the way these physicians understand and act. Can one assume that they will get the "proper" understanding, that it will "appropriately" inform their behavior? I am not suggesting that this series should have been embedded in a research project. I use the series as an example of how an educational issue can be recognized and then dealt with in a superficial manner that obscures rather than illuminates the ramifications of the issue, and, significantly, in a way that provides no empirical basis for learning more about an issue that all concerned admit is a crucial one. The Mayo Clinic did not achieve its reputation by researching important problems in this way, by starting with belief and hope and ending with belief and hope. But, one might ask, is not the series better than nothing? My answer is in the negative because it gives the appearance of appropriateness at the expense of trivializing, if not burying, the problem. And that brings me to the third aspect of the rationale for the series: the assumption that, despite the deficits in medical education with regard to people who are drug dependent, aged, or suicidal, physicians have the appropriate understanding, caring, and compassionate approach toward the patients they encounter in their specialties. The series does not and cannot challenge this assumption. But this series does have one clear virtue: it approaches, albeit incompletely and indirectly, recognition of a significant issue.

I said earlier that interest in and the desire to become a performer are necessary but not sufficient basis to be permitted to become a performer. Talent, I said, was a crucial ingredient. The purpose of this chapter was to make salient how the would-be performer needs to be helped, instructed, and supervised to capitalize on those features. That is by way of saying that the would-be performer has capital which can be productively exploited over the course of a career. As John Gielgud says so beautifully in his introduction to Stanislavski's book (1936), the process of exploitation is, at least, in regard to the performing actor, not taken with the seriousness that is required and, therefore, explains why so many theatrical performers lose whatever capital they may have had. Gielgud does not commit the error of misplaced emphasis: blaming only the actor who, he emphasizes, is embedded in a system of theatrical production (the theater generally) that is so frequently inimical to the growth of the performing artist. Yes, an individual artist may squander his or her talents, but more frequently it is the system we call *the* theater—its commercial aspects, its culture which reinforces individualism rather than collegiality, the poor quality of leadership, the lack of the desire for and availability of forums of critical appraisal—that Gielgud indicts:

> In spite of their self-centredness, actors are uncertain in their hearts, though they may appear boundlessly confident before an audience. A tactless director whom they do not wholly admire, or whom they think prejudiced or

personally hostile, can destroy their belief in themselves easily enough. Their knowledge is picked up haphazardly over many years, and they hardly dare to advise each other about acting because they feel that for every player the problem is a different one, a private secret to be jealously preserved. There are few set rules, except the most elementary—audibility, imagination, concentration. Actors fear lest they may become old fashioned and stilted on the one hand or slapdash and newfangled on the other. The basic craftsmanship— the five-finger exercises, the physical dexterity, the quickness of eye and hand and lips, these things are not easy to achieve. They are not practised or perfected in a daily routine as they are by executants of the sister arts, whether they are successful virtuosi or struggling beginners. Often players do not realise their own limitations or possibilities until they find themselves rehearsing a part which makes big demands upon them. Then they are not prepared— they lose their voices, find their costumes too heavy, their tongues become twisted in trying to sustain long speeches, they clip their words or find themselves out of breath. They do not excel in costume and modern dress to equal advantage—they are juveniles or character actors, but seldom both. Rarely are they equally at home in several different types of play. Stanislavski is aware of all these difficulties. He describes them vividly. He has tried to answer many questions. There are people who will say that his method is not practical for the commercial theatre. But this book is not a set textbook. It merely discusses difficulties, presents problems and suggests solutions. (p. i)

So, what about the teacher as performer? In the following chapters I seek to convince the reader that what I have said about performing artists is in all respects applicable to the classroom teacher. The venue is different, the audience is different, ultimate goals are different, the scripts (the curriculum) are different, but two things are not different; the teacher wants the audience of students to find that teacher interesting, stimulating, believable, someone who helps them see themselves and their world in a new and enlarged way, someone who satisfies their need for new experiences that take them out of their ordinary selves, someone they willingly come back to because they want to see the next act in a play about learning. And teachers teach in a system that only pays lip service to the necessity of their understanding what the teacher's role requires.

CHAPTER 5

The Teacher as Performer

National-social-cultural history has always provided the context determining people's choice of career. As that history documents, changes in that context perforce indicates changes in who chooses this or that career and why. So, for example, in earlier days, choosing a career in law, medicine, public service, and the ministry was very much determined by a person's social class, religion, color, and wealth; these professions were not, of course, anything resembling realistic choices for women. A career in the performing arts was regarded, if not as sinful, as a mark of a disdained peculiarity. The assassination of President Lincoln by an actor is testimony to the emergence of the performing arts in America, but it also played into the view that performing artists, like those in a circus, were a strange breed apart. It was recognized by the American educated elite that the performing arts had a long, popular, respected place in European countries, and it was seen as a sign of cultural growth and "high culture" when leading European, usually British, performing artists accepted invitations to display their artistry here. Nevertheless, it took a long time for a change in attitude to occur toward those who sought a career in the performing arts. And crucial in that change was the creation and financing of training centers by individuals in the American social-cultural-financial elite. Two things are deserving of emphasis for what comes later in this chapter. The first is that the creation of indigenous training-educational centers both mirrored and stimulated a change of attitude toward performing artists. That in large part explains why the creation of music schools and conservatories were first to appear: the performing musicians expressed a universal language that stirred and satisfied basic emotions in ways that did not raise issues of morality or appropriate lifestyle. The tie between music and religion was a historical fact and tradition. Music, by which was meant "classical" music, was uplifting to everyone, including children and the "weaker" sex. The culture, traditions, and subject matter of the theater were a different story. Much of the dramatic literature was not for everyone, certainly not for children and adolescents. It was a literature seen as frequently depicting ideas and relationships that were morally disturbing or sexually exciting or had endings which neither religion nor accepted criteria of what is right or wrong or in good taste should sanction. What I have said here is in all respects illustrated in the history of Hollywood which until three or so decades ago censored films to ensure that their themes, portrayals, and endings did not offend "accepted morality." The same situation obtained before there were movies.

The second point deserving emphasis is that actors (and later those in the dance) were seen as possessing a bohemian lifestyle, a perception and judgment that was not totally unjustified if by bohemian you mean that many of them had a counter-cultured stance reflected in outlook, lifestyle, a nonchalance about sexual relationships, and distinctive dress. Greenwich Village early on acquired the reputation for being a bohemian enclave populated and then dominated by flamboyant, "loose" types of artists.

If one were forced to point to one factor governing attitudes toward and judgments of performing artists, it was a devout religiosity. The earliest settlers described America as a Garden of Eden where virtue reigned until the counter-cultural Adam and Eve succumbed to the temptations of sin. Given that very early history, it was predictable that in America the performing arts (music-singing aside) would not be hospitably received. Choosing a career in these arts remained inconceivable for a very long time, there was no audience.

Two factors combined to ensure that teaching the young was both desirable and mandatory. Being able to read allowed one to read and absorb biblical morality and history. Sustaining a free and democratic fledgling society would be possible only if its citizens were literate, had computational skills, and an understanding of how America became and stood for what it is, was, and why. As I have indicated elsewhere (Sarason, 1998), there has been only one truly serious education president and that was Thomas Jefferson. Anyone who reads his writings on and accomplishments in matters educational will quickly grasp the centrality of teaching and teachers for America's future. Neither Jefferson nor anyone else at the time had any doubts on that score.

There were, of course, no centers for training teachers. Where would they come from? Who should be a teacher? What should be criteria for selection? What did the role of teacher mean? If necessity is the mother of invention, in this case, in those very early colonial days necessity dictated that one took what one could get, and that meant clerics and women who could read, write, and had knowledge of numbers and computational skills. Initially, teachers were mostly males. By the mid-nineteenth century that had discernibly begun to change; what today we call the elementary school became the province of women. There were far more elementary than secondary schools, the latter having more male teachers. But what some have called the "feminization" of schools was picking up steam. There were several reasons for that, but the one most relevant for my purposes is that women were seen, to put it in modern parlance, as more "with it" in regard to understanding young children and responsibly ensuring that their behavior was consistent with a clear, bedrock morality. Men had a similar responsibility, but in a largely agricultural society it was women who managed the home and reared children. The image of Mary with the Christ child was more than mere image. It encapsulated the view that women, more than men, were tender, compassionate, and sensitive. At the same time those virtues were the basis for seeing women as the "weaker" sex, and needing the strong hand of men to keep those virtues from corrupting excess; they nevertheless were seen as virtues for teaching—rearing children at home or in what was then a school. (Please note that controversy still exists today about the nature and sources of the differences between genders in regard to these virtues.) But this view of women as teachers was in the nature of an abstraction; it had no practical consequences. The criteria for hiring a teacher were that she was available, literate, of impeccable demeanor and morality, religiously devout, and willing to accept meager financial recompense. How the teacher taught was never spelled out. It was assumed that teaching was a relatively simple affair in which children learned what they needed to learn by rote memory and drill. The teacher was a technician, a conduit for conveying information and reinforcing a moral-religious outlook. If a child did not learn, it was a mark against the child, not a consequence of a teacher's inadequacy or pedagogy. It would not occur to parents to say their child was not learning because he or she was not "understood"; that possibility did not begin to take hold before the mid-nineteenth century.

What were the characteristics of women who sought to teach? There really is no good empirical basis for answering that question, but what little there is suggests that for some young women teaching was a respectable way of supporting an independent or semi-independent existence, especially if for one reason or another the economic status of her family was or had become marginal, this at a time when opportunities for gainful employment for women were, to say the least, few indeed. Then there were women who were spinsters or thought they would be spinsters for whom teaching would give them community status and provide satisfactions compensating for or ameliorating the loneliness of spinsterhood. And then there were those for whom teaching was seen as a way of contributing to the lofty goals of a new society whose future would be endangered if its young were uneducated. If the motivations to teach were undoubtedly mixed, teaching was never chosen over marriage and family as a career. To the extent women were exalted in society it was in their role as marriage partners and mothers. By law teaching terminated with marriage.

Matters did not change much until the latter half of the nineteenth century. A steady increase in population, the beginning waves of immigration, and legislation mandating compulsory education required a much larger pool of teachers. It was then that institutes, seminaries, and "normal schools" with one or sometimes 2-year programs for teachers began to sprout. Aside from exceptions I shall note shortly, these preparatory programs emphasized the technical aspects of pedagogy, the "how to do it" aspects. And those technical aspects rested on conceptions of children and learning not much more sophisticated than those of earlier days. It is only slightly unfair to say that children were perceived as empty vessels which it was the teachers obligation to fill, that left to their own devices children would lack habits of discipline and any desire to learn, that the learning process required a teacher who in relation to that process combined the authority of an executive, a legislative, and judiciary. The child was a passive, conforming, recipient of a teacher's knowledge and wisdom. Children needed to be tamed and socialized. It was as if the child was by nature an adversary of learning, law, and order. And nowhere was this conception seen as more necessary and relevant than in the ever growing urban areas to which immigrants flocked and in whose schools classes of 50 and more students were the norm. When at the close of the nineteenth century John Dewey described teachers as "commanders," he was underlining the similarity between military training and what he observed in the classroom, and by extension the counterproductive contents, methods, and theory of the pedagogy teachers were taught and absorbed. Teachers sought to control, not to understand, to instruct, not to elicit, to teach groups, not individuals. The fact and realities of individuality did not inform pedagogy. It was as if there were two theories of learning: one appropriate to adults, one appropriate to children. Children were a species apart, they did not need to be understood, they needed to be molded just as the potter molds his clay.

I am not being hypercritical of the preparatory programs for teachers that had emerged, and for two reasons. The first is that they were prisoners of their time, mirroring well the regnant conception of children and learning. To expect that they could or should have known or done better is projecting the present onto the past. The second reason is that teaching was not considered a profession in that it had no code of ethics, a demonstrated knowledge base, or a commitment to the pursuit of new knowledge, nor could its members determine the conditions in which they rendered service. A profession is one whose members have something to "profess."

What did teachers have to profess? The answers at the time were few and unpersuasive. At best teaching was considered an art. The more usual view was that teaching was a rather prosaic affair not requiring substantial knowledge or complex ways of conveying that knowledge. That as the decades of the nineteenth century passed women represented a sizeable majority of teachers played into the prejudice about the intellectual limitations of women. If women could perform a task, it clearly meant that the task could not be very intellectually complex or arduous! It is not happenstance that all but a very few centers preparing teachers had any relationship to colleges and universities which, needless to say, had not been hospitable to the admission of women.

Beginning around the middle of the nineteenth century there was a new development which by the end of the century very much changed conceptions about the nature and purposes of teaching, and that is because these conceptions centered around the capacities of children and the moral obligation of teachers to understand and exploit those capacities. Teaching was no prosaic affair; to understand and respond to children as individuals—to grasp the way the child thinks and feels—meant that teachers had to be able to recognize and identify the feelings and thought processes of children. The source of those conceptions was largely European theorists and practitioners whose work became known to some upper class American women dissatisfied with what schools were; and some of those Europeans visited this country and gave lectures and demonstrations. And it was also the case that these visits stimulated some of these women to visit and observe these foreign centers. A large ocean separated the United States from Europe, but it did not prevent the exchange of ideas. The fact is that European influences on American pedagogy were but one instance of a continuing European influence. It was also occurring in such fields as medicine, legal practice and theory, science, religion, and political theory. Commerce in the world of ideas was expanding.

In the last quarter of the nineteenth century there were two Americans whose ideas introduced a new focus that went beyond a narrow, impersonal, "how to do it" pedagogy. The first of these was G. Stanley Hall, a psychologist, who fathered, so to speak, the field of child and adolescent psychology. His research and writings did not stand up well over time, but they had the effect of alerting both the general public and the educational community to the view that teachers needed to know more and to understand better the school-age child. The second American, John Dewey, is quite another matter. To say that he still is a major influence is not an exaggeration, and there are educators and psychologists today, myself included, who assert that if the letter and spirit of his position had been taken seriously, schools would not have acquired the shortcomings they did. (Japan was the one country which, beginning in the 1920s, took Dewey seriously; Sato, 1992.) The staggering corpus of Dewey's writings defies brief summary, but for my present purposes the following points will have to suffice:

- *From their earliest days children are curious, questing, questioning, exploring organisms.* When they start school, they are not mindless, unorganized characters without awe and wonder about themselves, others, and the world. They are already budding scientists and artists.
- *The classroom should be a place where children's constructive characteristics are recognized and respected.* To put it negatively, one does not start with a predetermined curriculum that ignores individuality and from the start requires the child to set aside what is in his or her mind, instead to conform, to learn what grownups think he or she needs. If you do not start with where children are, you are beginning the process of extinguishing motivation for and interest in what society wants children to learn.
- *Children have assets for productive learning.* They have strengths, and you build on them. If they are viewed as empty vessels or as deficit-ridden—as organisms to be "filled" and deficits to be repaired—you will more often than not end up blaming the victim, i.e., proving you were right in the first place.
- *Schools are not preparation for life; they are life itself.* The classroom is a place where almost all the values and problems of life in a democracy come up, and if they are not discussed and reflected in teacher-student and student-student relationships, in how the classroom is structured and run, in its "constitution," then the children and the society are shortchanged. If you regard students as in dire need of taming and socialization, as if they are incapable of understanding and insensitive to the complexities of democratic living, then schools will be factories, production machines, a mockery of the democratic ethos.

It should be obvious from these points why Dewey was so critical of schools for their view of children, and critical of a school structure whose main "virtue" was to prepare students to take the role of ciphers in industry. No one needed to tell Dewey that industry was organized on the assumption that workers had no minds—besides which, if they had minds, they had better leave them at home. Dewey was not a fan of Henry Ford's. More than anyone else of his time, Dewey sought to protect the child's "life of the mind." He saw that the way industry viewed people and the way it was organized came with a high price and that someday that price would be seen as self-defeating. He was, of course, right.

Let us now continue with more of Dewey's position.

- *Teachers should not be "commanders" (Dewey's word) embodying the executive, legislative, and judicial branches of classroom government.* The central point was that commanders tell people what to do and how to do it; they are the fount of knowledge from which pours information and facts to be memorized. That was the polar opposite of the context that makes for productive learning. Filling empty vessels with facts should never be confused with communicating with active minds about what they know and want to know.
- *The role of the teacher is one of coaching, managing, and arranging the learning environment.* This role appears messy in contrast to one where the teacher is essentially a well-meaning autocrat. It is a role ever sensitive to individual and group needs and changes, i.e., unpredictability is to be expected and not to be seen as interference with routine.
- *It is the obligation of the teacher to establish a relationship with parents.* Teachers need to realize that a parent has knowledge, is an asset, and has rights that should be respected. Parents are not foreign intruders but part of the enterprise. They can be valuable assets—but not if you see them as "just" parents.
- *Teacher-teacher and teacher-administrator relationships need to reflect the same mutual respect and attentiveness as teacher-student and teacher-parent relationships.* Dewey saw all of these relationships as generally lacking the features that make learning and growth more than a sometime thing. He regarded his psychological rationale for productive development in children to be totally applicable, morally and intellectually, to all stakeholders in the educational scene.
- *A school and school system exist in a community.* The community contains human and material resources about which school personnel *and* students should have working knowledge so that those resources can be tapped for educational purposes. The boundaries between school and society should be porous. The more schools are encapsulated places— the more the individual classroom is isolated from the rest of the school and the community—the more completely potential resources remain just that: potential, unmined, unconnected to the education of children.

Although he never put it in these terms, it is obvious that Dewey regarded the teacher as a performer, someone who took on or manifested characteristics considered necessary to affect her audience in specified ways, and, indeed, to meet their expectations of what a teacher should be like and how an audience should respond. From the standpoint of the teacher, the audience needed and expected her to "act" the way she did.

And if she did not act believably and consistently in that way, her audience would be unable to discharge well their obligations in the role as learners. In those days, and to a somewhat lesser degree today, the fear that haunted teachers, especially early in their careers, was being unable to maintain discipline, law, and order, and, therefore, subvert her believability in the well-defined role as a performer called teacher. It is worthy of emphasis that the audience expected the teacher to be a "commander," and if she was a poor commander, she would lose the control and respect of her troops; major or minor rebellions would occur, God forbid. (That is why men predominated in the emerging secondary schools. *They* could "control" the older child, they were figures of power and authority in ways that the "weaker sex" was not.)

No one "dreamed up" this conception of the role of teacher. Teachers taught the way they were taught when they were in school, and, with few exceptions, programs preparing them for a career in teaching reinforced this conception. Dewey's writings changed the rhetoric about the teacher's role, the contents and organization of the curriculum, the importance of taking the individuality of students into account, and the purposes of schooling, but it was largely rhetoric. Preparatory programs changed little, if at all. Matters were not helped any by Dewey's failure to address several questions which his position made salient. Who should be selected and be encouraged and permitted to be a teacher? By what criteria should such a process be governed? To what extent and in what ways can a preparatory program ensure that a would-be teacher has absorbed a genuine understanding of the changed conception of a learning process which centers on the assets, interests, motivations, and curiosity of children, a process which dramatically alters the performing role of teachers? What is meant, on what basis should we conclude, that a teacher recognizes, respects, and adapts to the individual differences in her audience? These and similar questions arise from Dewey's position. They are the opposite of trivial questions because they are a subset of the more general question: In close and intimate relationships how do we want people to know and act toward each other? For my purposes here the questions are: How do we want students and teachers to know, understand, and regard each other? What allows each to be believable to the other? Dewey does not leave you in doubt that possessing a theory of the "minds" of children is other than a first step for a teacher; acting appropriately and consistently with that theory is the ultimate litmus test, and we use the word *acting* (as we conventionally do) to acknowledge that the teacher is playing a role, adopting a psychological stance she does not ordinarily assume when she is not teaching. The maxim that a teacher teaches children, not subject matter, is *not* a downgrading of subject matter but a way of saying that if you do not understand where children are coming from in the classroom context, the intended meaning, significance, and utility of that subject matter may not be grasped.

I urge the reader to study Garrison's *Dewey and Eros* (1997), the subtitle of which is "Wisdom and desire in the art of teaching." In a most scholarly manner he makes it quite clear that Dewey rejects a kind of faculty psychology which leads to a conception of learning in which thinking, feeling, and desire-passion are for all practical purposes in distinct realms of the learning experience in *student and teacher*. It is not a rejection on principle but rather on the basis that *they are never separate in experience*. The early chapters of Garrison's may be hard going for some readers because he uses familiar terms in unfamiliar but historically justified ways. It is in the last three chapters, especially the one about a child named Tony Mitchell, that the reader will see why I suggested reading the book Garrison writes about passion, a word we ordinarily do not associate with teaching. It was implicitly and explicitly central to Dewey's conception of learning and thinking. In this connection the reader will find Robert Fried's *The Passionate Teacher* (1995) most instructive because of the compelling, concrete, and detailed examples he presents. Let me present an excerpt from what he calls the Prologue of his book.

> To be a passionate teacher is to be someone in love with a field of knowledge, deeply stirred by issues and ideas that challenge our world, drawn to the dilemmas and potentials of the young people who come into class each day—or captivated by all of these. A passionate teacher is a teacher who breaks out of the isolation of a classroom, who refuses to submit to apathy or cynicism. I argue in these pages that only when teachers bring their passions about learning and about life into their daily work can they dispel the fog of passive compliance or active disinterest that surrounds so many students. I believe that we all have it within ourselves to be passionate teachers, and that nothing else will quite do the trick.
>
> As adults working with young people, our passions are key to their engagement. For almost thirty years, working in primary, secondary, undergraduate, and graduate schools, I have been polishing John Dewey's argument that nothing much of lasting value happens in a classroom unless students' minds are engaged in ways that connect with their experience. But I have learned that just talking to people about engagement doesn't work: one has to *engage* people first.
>
> This book is the product of my struggle to do just that, to move from being a purveyor of good advice about teaching and learning to becoming an advocate for my own and other people's passionate approach to our work with students. It is much easier to give sermons on what ought to be than to put these notions into practice. So I rely, in these pages, on the stories and insights of a number of teachers who have inspired me. After many years of working with teachers and staff in their school settings, I have again joined

the ranks of full-time teachers, albeit at a university; I am now trying very hard to put this philosophy to work in my own classes.

For students to *engage* is not what is usually called "time on task": responding to work-sheets, recalling facts or dates, or reading chapters of a text and answering questions at the end. I want students to engage the way the clutch on a car gets engaged: an engine can be running, making appropriate noises, burning fuel and creating exhaust fumes, but unless the clutch is engaged, nothing moves. It's all sound and smoke, and nobody gets anywhere.

In too many classrooms we see the sound and smoke of note-taking, answer-giving, homework-checking, test-taking, and the forgetting that so quickly follows. In the end, there is creativity and excitement for the few, compliance and endurance for most, rebellion and failure for some; but not very much work of high quality is being produced, and not much intense engagement of the mind and spirit takes place.

A number of years ago, Tim Sullivan, a fourth-grade teacher here in Concord, New Hampshire, asked his class how they felt about a bill before the state legislature to raise from three years to twelve the age under which use of seat belts would be required:

"We decided to adopt the bill as a class project. We debated it in class, coached by a high school student who was on the debating team. The kids also contacted a pro-seat belt group who sent someone to talk to them and brought along a seat-belt car crash simulator, called 'The Convincer.' My students invited our mayor, city council, school board, and several legislators, who came to our class to listen to the kids and take a ride on the Convincer.

Every student then wrote to the state legislators and 85 percent of them wrote back with personalized notes. When it came time for legislative hearings, I asked my kids if they wanted to testify before subcommittees of the House and the Senate. I thought I'd have to lean on them to volunteer, but every hand went up. And the kids found that because they had done their homework, they were able to respond to the legislators' questions and win their respect.

The bill passed both houses, and when Governor Sununu vetoed it, the kids lobbied hard for the over-ride motion, which made it through the House and would have succeeded in the Senate if the governor hadn't personally intervened. We lost in the Senate by one vote. The kids were disappointed, but we knew all along we might lose. The whole point was to understand the process. Those kids came away with a better sense of how a bill becomes law than any class I've ever taught."

By way of comparison, I want to look at the selection of candidates for the profession of medicine. There are many readers of this book who can relate "war stories" about this or that type of physician who had the interpersonal style of a tank or the coldness of ice, or who confused the use of technical jargon with informative communication, or whose display of caring and compassion was notable for its absence. In the past three decades the increase in malpractice suits has markedly escalated, an increase that is not unrelated to a sullen ambivalence of many people to physicians. Some lawyers have commented that more than a few malpractice suits arise less from poor judgment than from the physician's interpersonal style. "Doctors are human, they can make mistakes, but I cannot tolerate being treated like an ignoramus who has an empty head, has no right to ask questions or challenge him, who alone makes decisions about what my options are"—that, my lawyer friends tell me, tips some patients in the direction of a malpractice suit. And, as polls have shown, no longer are physicians accorded the very high standing they once enjoyed. All of this should occasion no surprise because there is nothing, literally nothing, among the criteria for admission to medical school which has any meaningful bearing on the individual's caring, compassionate behavior. And as has been often noted, once the individual is admitted, the culture of the medical school and hospital works against the display of caring and compassionate behavior. It has long been an open secret that physicians look down on their psychiatric colleagues and consider them as second or third rate doctors (and some have said to me they are really not doctors) because they spend their time trying to understand "symptoms" in terms of the patient's thinking, feelings, family context—a kind of hell diving the ordinary physician regards as unnecessary.

Despite Dewey and others who came after him, it is still the case that, like medical education, the criteria for the selection of teachers are unrelated to those characteristics a teacher should have if he or she is to perform in a role requiring not only a book knowledge of child development but also the capacity to use that role to understand, intuit, flush out how a child sees him or herself in the learning context. We are not born with that capacity, and if we know anything, it is that because of life experiences and differences in temperament people differ wildly in those characteristics. Just as not everyone who wants to be a doctor should be encouraged or even allowed to begin that career, the same holds for people who want to be teachers. That assertion, one could argue, is unfair because it assumes that we know how to select for those characteristics, or that procedures to improve selection would be sufficiently valid to justify their use, or that I am vastly underestimating the positive impact of preparatory programs in helping candidates develop those characteristics. It is true that we do not at present know how to select on those characteristics. It is also true that developing valid screening procedures will be neither quick or easy. I agree there is a moral issue here: You should not employ procedures with a low or dubious validity that will screen out too many of those who may have those characteristics. That is to say, the procedures have to demonstrate that among those selected there are few false negatives. *But at present we are employing no procedures relevant to these characteristics, as is similarly the case in medical education.* The problem was not taken off the agenda; it has never been on the agenda. That is why in 1962 we (Sarason, Davidson, & Blatt) entitled our book *The Preparation of Teachers: An Unstudied Problem in Education.* And that is why in 1996 the *National Commission on Teaching and America's Future* (under Dr. Linda Darling-Hammond's direction) issued a report as critically damning of the selection and preparation of teachers as has ever been written. The report was not written by "outsiders" taking dead aim on their favorite target: teachers. It was written and signed by experienced educators courageous enough to say the emperor is naked. Anyone who reads that report will be unable to say that I am vastly underestimating the positive impact of preparatory programs. Nevertheless, that report glosses over the nature and complexity of the phenomenology of *performing*: How and why it requires a teacher to think, feel, intuit, and flexibly adapt to students' individuality, and to do all of this for the purpose of engendering understanding and a sense of growth. When we say that performers seek both to instruct and *move* an audience, we mean that the teacher as performing artist has in some positive way altered the students' conception of the relationship between sense of self and the significance of subject matter, i.e., an increase in competence. And it is that process and engagement which reinforces the sense of the teacher's competence. The word *instruct* engenders imagery of a one-way-street interaction, imagery all too frequently observable in the classroom, which is why so many students never experience the sense of being *moved*. If this point is not central in the preparatory program of the teacher, it subverts all other changes or improvements a program can make. That is why it is irresponsible and unfair to blame teachers. They are victims.

The written word is by no means adequate to convey the issue I have been discussing. What gets conveyed when I say that how a teacher defines and performs the role tells us how he or she understands the mind set of the young audience? What gets conveyed when I say that when the understanding is narrow, superficial, and insensitive, he or she may be totally unaware that the performance has had counterproductive consequences even though some or most of the audience appears to have learned what was hoped they would? That is to say, the operation was a success but part of each student's hopes, needs, and motivations withered. What gets conveyed when it is said that the teacher has to be able to identify with the learner: Where he or she is coming from, where the teacher has to start if the student's understanding of the "story" of learning is to be enlarged? In his legendary *Talks to Teachers on Psychology and to Students on Some of Life's Ideals* William James (1902) in his truly inimitable way touches on aspects of these questions far better than I have or could, but the meaning of his words, the imagery he sought to depict, were not comprehended.

I urge the reader to see the film or get the video *Mr. Holland's Opus*. It doesn't say it all, it *shows* it all. Mr. Holland, no youngster, is a musician-composer who for economic and family reasons "becomes" a teacher, presumably after being "credentialed." Steeped in the traditions and values of classical music, Mr. Holland sees his role as instilling in his audience of high school students an appreciation of "good"music. If his audience of students had a knowledge of or interest in such music was not something to which he gave any thought. His role, to him a glimpse of the obvious, was to instill in his audience an appreciation of such music, and by appreciation he meant it in its dictionary sense: to *increase* or enlarge in personal value, certainly not to remain the same or depreciate. When Mr. Holland sees that his audience is unresponsive to his teachings, he does not ask himself why, but he becomes more hortatory and resentful. But the students sit there passively with looks of contempt on their faces. It is a disaster, to the point where he seeks help from others (a friendly teacher, the principal). They are not helpful. Indeed, the friendly teacher reinforces Mr. Holland's opinion that high school students want coddling and entertainment, not a struggle with learning. One day, as a result of a one-on-one interaction with a dispirited, unmusical student, Mr. Holland has an "aha" experience: It hits him with hurricane force that he had never had an inkling of what this girl thought and felt. *Now* he understood her, *now* he knew her. The rest of the film shows how this epiphany causes him radically to redefine his role, methods, and acting style, with the result that the students become alive, interested, and productive. The first half of the film depicts a context of unproductive learning, the second half a context of productive learning. In the first half he is a hapless, ineffective, sleep-producing performer; In the second half his performance is at the Oscar level. (I will have more to say about this film in later chapters.)

Mr. Holland was prepared to teach the way I am prepared to go to the moon. The movie does not tell us how over the years he had obtained credentials to devote a career to music and musical composition. Nor does the film tell us on what basis he was credentialed to be a teacher, but whatever that basis it was irresponsibly inadequate. That he knew his subject matter is incontestable. That he mightily and desperately strove to "communicate" a subject matter he loved is also incontestable. That he had not the foggiest notion of how to understand students so that he would know where and how to start with them is also incontestable. He acted like some parents do when one day they decide that their child needs to be toilet trained. They promptly begin to "teach" the child in a serious, no-nonsense way, get puzzled when after a week or 2 the child shows no interest or improvement, they become more serious and pressuring, and on and on in what becomes a battle in a way from which no one escapes psychological injury. You could argue that the comparison is misleading because the two instances are extreme cases. They may be extreme, but they are not infrequent. However, the point of the comparison is that the inadequacies of Mr. Holland's preparation and approach are the norm even though their overt consequences are not as obviously dramatic as in his case. There is good evidence that as students go from elementary to middle to high school their boredom with, disaffection from, and lack of motivation for learning increase. The awe, wonder, curiosity with which children start schooling is, generally speaking, absent or markedly reduced when they are graduated from high school. Over the decades I have observed and talked to and interviewed hundreds of school teachers (as well as their students), and it has come as no surprise to me that more formal studies confirmed my personal conclusions and the basic point *Mr. Holland's Opus* illustrates. Teachers, again generally speaking, perform in a way and on a basis that turns off their audiences. In the theater the actor, despite immersion in and identification with a particular role, is acutely sensitive to audience reaction, to any sign that the audience finds his or her portrayal convincing in the intended way. And after opening night the actor waits anxiously for the next day when the newspaper critics will pass judgment on the play and its performers. Some plays close very quickly; there is no opportunity to try to learn from the failure. It is different with the classroom teacher who has the same audience each day. The teacher does not worry about whether the audience will return. The audience, by law and parental authority, *must* return. The teacher has the opportunity to change her way of interpreting her role depending on how she perceives and interprets audience reaction. But what do we mean by perceiving and interpreting? Mr. Holland had countless opportunities to change and interpret audience reaction. He did interpret them and concluded that the problem was in the minds of the audience; *they* did not understand and appreciate *him*. That it was the other way around could not occur to him, nothing in his preparation alerted him to the fact that his role obligated him to perform in a way to make it believable to students that he was sincerely interested in their thoughts, feelings, reactions, suggestions. It was only after repeated failure and frustration, after he was, so to speak, hit over the head, that he saw his audience in a new light, a light for which he had never been prepared.

I made it my business to ask every educator I met who had seen the movie how they felt about it. I probably asked upwards of 50 people. Although a few said Mr. Holland was an extreme but not rare case, everyone said that the basic point of the film was valid. And at least half of them spontaneously went on to say that preparatory programs for teachers were blatantly deficient in helping teachers to understand and to devise means for understanding students other than in superficial ways. That critical assessment has been made by teachers ever since formal preparatory programs came into existence as a legally sanctioned way to "professionalize" teaching, to be no more than an agency to credential those seeking such a career.

This chapter has centered around four themes. First, as with any performing artist, the teacher willingly and internally defines a role with characteristics intended to elicit in an audience of students a set of reactions that will move them willingly to persist in the pursuit of new knowledge and skills. Second, the way in which the teacher defines and seeks *to appear* in his or her role contains a "picture" of what the members of that audience needs, thinks, feels, hopes for, expects, deserves, and that constitutes and defines what a teacher understands. Third, in the modal classroom there is a disjunction—the opposite of a meeting of the minds—between that understanding and what the audience experiences. Fourth, preparatory programs, their rhetoric aside, ill prepare teachers in regard to their role, the disjunction, and ways to deal with it.

These themes have hardly been taken seriously. The emphasis, especially in recent years, has been on subject matter; as if acquiring subject matter is more important, incomparably more important, than how the student audience experiences, utilizes, and values that subject matter. This "shape up or ship out" mentality is mostly held by those who view what they pejoratively call the "child centered" approach as a mischievous, subversive, or digressive undercutting of the overarching goal of acquiring subject matter. It is a mentality intended to remind teachers that they should define their role and that of their audiences as the learning of subject matter. The performance of the teacher will be judged by agents external both to the teacher and the audience. On the level of rhetoric they might agree that this requires artistry, that the teacher is not an impersonal, mindless conduit for information. But what that artistry consists of, how it should appear to or impact on the audience, how that artistry is learned, how and why the different contents and styles of artistry have different consequences—about all of these the critics are at best vague and at worst silent, leaving me, at least, with two conclusions: They have never examined their own classroom experiences, and/or their current experience with and knowledge of classrooms is nil. For all practical purposes, they do not see the teacher as a performing artist with an audience but as a semi-mechanic. And some of these critics are the most enthusiastic proponents of the view that computer technology in the classroom is God's gift to the stimulation and enlivenment of students' interest in absorbing subject matter. When, as I predict, this technology will not receive the degree of confirmation these enthusiasts expect, they will undoubtedly come up with other equally dubious panaceas, as well as new or old scapegoats.

So let me state, as I have in my previous writings, my judgment on the importance of subject matter. Subject matter is of bedrock importance, and for two reasons. The first is that subject matter is the only basis for comprehending a society's past and present; without it a person is robbed of knowledge of how one's world has the features, good and bad, that it has. It is a knowledge of man's accomplishments, glories, villainies, hopes, disappointments, strivings, and more. It is a past that has shaped our present from which will emerge a future the outlines of which we can only dimly predict. Second, subject matter—whether it be mathematics, science, history, literature—has *practical* utility because it can inform how one works and how one lives one's life. Subject matter never developed in an encapsulated world of its own but rather as efforts to understand the world, and that is no less true for understanding and applying subject matter today. The more one is ignorant of subject matter, or comes to view it as arid and irrelevant, the more one is imprisoned in a narrow social and personal world. The intention of this chapter was an emphasis on the obvious: The way subject matter is taught and experienced by students ensures that students will tune in or turn off. Although the themes in this chapter are by no means new, they have been far from the center of educational theory, research, and practice, and they are even farther from what powers preparatory programs. Over 50 years ago Arthur Jersild (1955) dealt with them in his book *When Teachers Face Themselves*. It is a book based on a variety of studies Jersild conducted with teachers. To give an idea of what Jersild's book contains, here are three extended quotations.

> All of the work that has preceded this book—in classrooms with children, in conferences with teachers, in the literature dealing with the theoretical issues involved—has emphasized one fact. The teacher's understanding and acceptance of himself is the most important requirement in any effort he makes to help students to know themselves and to gain healthy attitudes of self-acceptance. The crucial question that has emerged again and again is this: What does this effort to help students mean in a distinctly intimate, personal way in the teacher's own life? This book endeavors to explore some of the issues that must be explored when we seek an answer to this question.
>
> It has become increasingly clear over the years, as the work in this inquiry proceeded, that self-understanding requires something quite different from the methods, study plans, and skills of a "know-how" sort that are usually emphasized in education. Methods and techniques, group work, role playing, and other devices are useful at certain points. But these educational techniques are not what is primarily needed. They can be used merely as a

kind of external manipulation. When so used, they do not further and may even defeat the purpose we are seeking there. What is needed is a more personal kind of searching, which will enable the teacher to identify his own concerns and to share the concerns of his students. (p. 3)

The search for meaning is, as has been said, a distinctly personal search. It is not just a scholarly enterprise, although the pursuit of learning is an important aspect of it. It can be shared, to some extent, with others, and people can draw encouragement from the fact that others, like them, feel uneasy about the emptiness of much of what is done in the name of learning. But the real encounter with the problem must take place in the privacy of each person's own life. Even then, as D.H. Lawrence has pointed out, the meaning a person can embrace within his known self may be only a little clearing in the forest. But a little clearing is infinitely greater than no clearing at all, and it is better (according to the philosophy underlying this book) to dwell in such a clearing, and to work in it, with things that count, than just to go through the motions. It is better to have such a home in the wilderness than to move through life in a mechanical way, unreached, untouched, and unmoved by what one learns and uninvolved in what one teaches. (p. 7)

If we as educators are to face the problem of meaninglessness, we must make an effort to conduct education in depth—to move toward something that is personally significant beyond the facade of facts, subject matter, logic, and reason behind which human motives and a person's real struggles and strivings are often concealed. This does not mean the rejection of subject matter—far from it—but it does mean helping the learner to relate himself to what he is learning and to fit what he learns into the fabric of his life in a meaningful way.

Such an endeavor means an effort to overcome the prevailing tendency in education to encourage the learner to understand everything except himself.

It means an effort to achieve a better integration of thinking and feeling on the part of both children and adults.

It means an effort to cut through the pretense of "interest" in learning, which children and adults so widely adopt in order to conform or to escape disapproval from their elders. It means also that the process of learning will not be used as a means of competing with others and gaining power over them.

Actually, each subject that is taught in elementary or high school or college could, in one way or another, for certain learners, be deeply charged with meaning. Each subject could, in one way or another, help some young person discover his skills and explore or use his resources.

But much of what teachers have to learn, much of what they have to teach, and much of what the millions of pupils who attend our schools are compelled to study is not meaningful but meaningless, largely because we have assumed that knowledge has value apart from its meaning for the one who acquires it. When we consider the problem of meaningless, it is not extreme to say that one of the basic troubles in education is that as educators we have not had the courage to face the personal implications of our calling. (pp. 80–81)

Jersild's central theme can be put in this way: A teacher has to learn to use his or her life as a source of understanding the student's thoughts, feelings, and attitudes toward learning. When he says you should teach children, not subject matter, he is not downgrading subject matter but rather indicating that in a context of productive learning subject matter should be experienced as personally meaningful and reinforcing of the maxim that the more you know the more you must know, there is no end point. Jersild was probably unacquainted with Stanislavski's *An Actor Prepares*. He would have felt kinship with him.

To some readers it may seem that Jersild and I are proponents of a touchy-feely pedagogy or conception of learning. I have come to expect that as soon as I say that productive learning of subject matter is both a personal and interpersonal affair in which thinking, feeling, attitudes, and purposes are indissolubly present. Any conception of learning which does not take that seriously and, in addition, tells or suggests to us what that means for the teacher as performer, as instructor and mover, is literally unrealistic and is defeating the purpose of schooling. Like it or not, and some do not like it, the teacher as performing artist is faced with a terribly complex and difficult task that all those in the conventional performing arts confront: How do you put yourself into a role and then enact it in ways that instruct and move an audience, fulfilling the expectation of the audience that they have in some way learned something about themselves and their world? They have been moved, they seek more such experiences. Teachers are not born, so to speak with such attributes. It requires a kind of training which no preparatory program I know has taken seriously, if at all, which is why these attributes play no role in the admission of candidates to these programs. And when to that you add the fact that the size, structure, and culture of schools are the opposite of conducive to the display of these attributes, it is truly a case of adding insult to injury, which means, of course, that both teachers and students are the victims.

The reader will be disappointed if he or she expects that I will lay out a set of concrete proposals for the selection and training of teachers. I have learned the hard way that before you proclaim your answers to a new and complex problem, you had better personally implement and experience what those presumed truths look like in action. (At age 80 I am in no position to do that!) I will offer some suggestions. But of one thing I am sure: We have a lot to learn from those who are part of training programs in the conventional performing arts.

CHAPTER 6

The Classroom and the School Culture

When I was in graduate school (after the Civil War), I bought a used book with the arresting title *Know Your Mind* by Dr. Charles B. Psycho. The first sentence was, "As a child I was very young." Dr. Psycho went on to say that if you want to understand human behavior, you've bought the right book. But, he cautions, the reader first has to know something about the human brain. So he presents a drawing of the human brain and its lobes: frontal, occipital, temporal, parietal. And smack in the middle, with borders to these lobes, is a circle labeled "Poland." (My thesis advisor borrowed the book and never returned it.)

If you were to make a serious drawing of our educational system, the teacher would be the equivalent of Poland, except, of course, the drawing would depict the central message that all parts of the system have as their major function, whether explicit or implicit, direct or indirect, to influence what a teacher says or does in the classroom. Parents, school administrators, boards of education, the legislative and executive branches of local and state governments, the state departments of education, departments of education in colleges and universities—these are the parts of the educational system (or brain), the activities of which impact on teachers, an impact which may be immediate or delayed, small or large, clear or murky, controversial or benign, critical or supportive. You cannot see the system the way you see a rock or a box; a system has to be conceptualized, it is not a *thing*. Unlike the human brain which has fantastically coordinated parts, the educational system is markedly uncoordinated; one part may be at cross purposes with one or another part, one part may not "hear" the messages of the other parts.

What we ordinarily call a school system is a subsystem in a larger educational system which influences and puts constraints on the local school system. The purposes, organizational structures, record keeping, modes of accountability, and substance and scope of curricula of the local school system are literally incomprehensible apart from the larger educational system in which it is embedded. This is not to say that the local system is a mere pawn of that larger system, but rather that it is far from independent of it.

In this chapter I restrict myself to the single school in the local system because from the standpoint of the teacher it is the single school and the local system of which the teacher is most aware and concerned. Indeed, although teachers know in the abstract that there is a larger system, they are unsophisticated about how the larger system has shaped what they say or do in the classroom. Level of sophistication increases as you go up the administrative hierarchy of the local system. From the standpoint of the teacher, it is the school and the local system that affects performance and state of professional well-being. All else is far in the background, even though in an ultimate sense many of the educational changes which teachers advocate (or fantasize about) require initiatives and changes in the larger system.

I said earlier that the local school and school system are incomprehensible apart from the larger educational system. Given my focus on the teacher, the principle undergirding that assertion is no less applicable to the teacher. When we observe a teacher in the classroom, our attention is riveted on the teacher and the students in an encapsulated physical space, and the interpretations we make and the conclusions we draw are almost always about *that* teacher and *those* students, as if the rest of the school and school system has not played (or are not playing) a role. A moment's reflection tells us, however, that even before we enter the classroom we know, theoretically and otherwise, that what we will see will in some ways bear the imprimatur of that school and local system. Those ways may not be apparent, they may be apparent but subtle, they may be blatant, but never absent. Teachers know that. For example, on numerous occasions I have asked teachers two questions. The first was, Would what you say, do, or feel in the classroom be the same in any other similarly graded classroom in another school in your school system? The second question was, Would you say, do, or feel the way you do regardless of which school system you were in? No teacher said yes to either question. It was, they said, obvious that schools and school systems differed markedly in their influence on teacher thinking and behavior; no teacher would willingly take a position in another school system without endeavoring to find out what life was like in it. As one teacher put it, "I know what my life is like in my school, the balance of the pluses and minuses, and before I go elsewhere I have to determine the nature of that balance there, although you really never know what life is like elsewhere until you teach there." What these teachers were acknowledging was identical to what performing artists have long known:

Behind the stage and off in the wings is an assortment of people who, for good or for bad, play a role in their performance. We in the audience, like the observer in the classroom, do not see those external "players," but the performing teacher and artists know they are a living, influential presence.

Beginning with Waller's 1932 book there have been thousands of books describing how the culture of the school and school system intrudes into a teacher's sense of self, competency, purpose, independence, and well-being. I shall make no attempt to review this literature. Instead, I shall give two examples which convey facets the reader may find helpful in gaining an understanding of the main point of this chapter.

Before World War II teacher's unions were not an important force on the educational scene. (That was not the case for unions in some of the performing arts.) Teachers viewed themselves as professionals, not as "workers." They, on the surface at least, passively complied to the rules, regulations, and dictates of the principal and others in the administrative hierarchy. Their salaries, duties, and working conditions were decided by others in a top-down style. Teachers, of course, had diverse grievances, but it was a case of the single teacher vs. all those in superior administrative positions of power. In principle, the single teacher could "bargain" with administrators, but it was like a mouse vs. a lion. After World War II the situation began steadily to change so that by 1960 militant teacher's unions were above, not below, the educational horizon and in short order they become a potent force. How to explain this? There can be no doubt that immorally low salaries were a major factor. But that factor masked a volcano of grievances, long-festering, that can be summed up in two words: lack of respect and impotence. Money was historically-sociologically a proxy for the lack of respect bordering on contempt that school officialdom was seen by teachers as conveying. That it was a proxy was confirmed in one of Albert Shanker's columns in the *New York Times* years after the unions had become a major force in school systems. He asked if the time had come when unions had to bargain for more than "bread and butter" issues consistent with traditional unionism, and to put educational policy and management on the bargaining table. He was in effect saying that education was too important to be left solely in the hands of the generals and that those on the firing lines had to be given voice. Neither then nor later did Shanker elaborate publicly on that theme. Privately it was another matter. In several long meetings I had with him he made no bones about several things. First, despite the successes of the unions, officialdom still viewed teachers as proletarians incompetent to have a voice in substantive educational decision making; the teacher's turf was the classroom, and only the top administrators had the knowledge and wisdom about substantive issues. Second, and related to the first, schools were organized and run by people whose knowledge of classrooms and teachers' experience, problems, and advice was limited, in addition to which these higher-ups made token gestures to provide forums which would allow teachers safely to express their views. No one had to tell Shanker that schools and school systems were riddled by diverse forms of adversarialisms which negatively affected how a teacher felt and performed in the classroom. Third, when officialdom instituted (= mandated) educational changes which altered what a teacher did in the classroom and those changes were feckless in their consequences, as they usually were, failure was attributed to teacher resistance, rigidity, and unimaginativeness, not to unilateral decision making, self-defeating processes of implementation, and unrealistic time tables. Fourth, Shanker did not need to be convinced by anyone that preparatory programs for educators, especially for teachers, were substantively, intellectually, and professionally at best superficial and at worst charades. When he talked about this point, I was startled. Why, I asked him, had he never said anything about that in his columns? And his answer was that many members of his union were faculty members in those programs; he could not publicly criticize those members and expect to remain president of the union. I refrained from pointing out that he was in the same position as teachers: if you spoke out, if you criticized, if you rocked the boat, you could be tossed overboard.

I consider Shanker both a heroic and a tragic figure. Heroic because no one more than he sought to convince teachers that they could not, must not, view themselves as impotent persons depending unrealistically for a sense of self-respect on those up on the hill in Kafka's Castle: those who view teachers as pawns in a chess game in which everybody experiences checkmate. Tragic because he knew that teachers were, generally speaking, ill prepared to understand and cope with a school culture containing factors which subtly and/or blatantly affect negatively the quality of a teacher's performance. He knew that, but he could not speak out.

If the performance of *any* performing artist is not independent of the organization that employs the artist, no performing artist is, again generally speaking, as negatively impacted upon as teachers are. Let me illustrate this with a personal experience which most readers have not been able or will not be able to duplicate: To observe, to get to know, to talk candidly with teachers over a 7-year period. For each of those years I twice visited two schools in Tucson, Arizona, in connection with Dr. Paul Heckman's project in Latino ghetto schools. Each visit was of 3 or 4 days duration.[1]

---

1. In 1996 Dr. Heckman edited a book *The Courage to Change* containing almost entirely accounts by teachers of their experience in the project. Dr. Viki Montera's doctoral dissertation (1997) gives added force and confirmation to the contents of teacher accounts. A much more comprehensive book on this very instructive project is being prepared by Heckman and Montera.

When the project began, the teachers and the principals saw themselves as coping with overwhelming problems deriving from an unsafe neighborhood, an unresponsive and unsupportive bureaucracy, many parents who could not speak comprehensible English, a large percentage of children who spoke better Spanish than English. These were not chaotic schools. They were schools under daily stress. Their personnel had not yet thrown in the towel, but they were not far from that point. They knew they were in trouble, and they embraced the project the major goal of which was to get school personnel and parents to assume the responsibility for changing the schools, a goal the project would support in diverse ways. It took 2 years before the staff truly believed that they and the parents were being given responsibility to make changes they saw fit; they were not used to such freedom and responsibility.

By the end of the project dramatic changes had taken place, but the one most salient for my purposes here is how the teachers came to see themselves as creative performers in the classroom who had loads of support and encouragement from the parents, principals, project staff, and the neighborhood. They had a sense of personal, interpersonal, professional growth heretofore relegated to private hope and fantasy. They also had a new sense of "audience" and their obligations to it.

To get permission to initiate the project from top officialdom was not easy. When officials finally approved the project, it was not because they understood it. They did not understand even though its rationale was given to them in spoken and in written form. They knew that the schools in those ghetto districts were inadequate, but they had no plans or ideas for what they could do. The administrative responsibility became that of the district supervisor. And that is when Lady Luck made her entrance: Elaine Rice grasped and enthusiastically supported the project's nontraditional rationale and, crucially, knew that her major contribution would be to *protect* it from an administrative culture and hierarchy that was fearful of departures from tradition. In the history and politics of Tucson and its school system, the governing rules were "don't rock the boat," "don't do anything that might offend and cause articulate segments of the community to criticize the schooling system." Dr. Rice—a very bright, highly educated, well-spoken, Boston-bred African American with unexcelled street smarts—became the intermediary between the project and what I call the "organizational craziness" of large institutional systems in general and school systems in particular (Sarason & Lorentz, 1998). While her role was a source of comfort, it was also a source of anxiety. What if she decided that her position as district supervisor was too frustrating, too demanding of her time and energy and she looked favorably on retirement or another position less taxing on her physical well-being? The answer was clear: the chances that the powers that be would appoint someone of her wisdom and resolution were slightly above zero. And that is precisely what happened in the seventh year of the project. Decisions were then made which undercut the project's achievements and continuation. And no group felt the negative impact more than teachers whose morale plummeted as their fond memories of what had been were tinged with sadness as stultifying tradition reasserted itself. They continued to "perform" but under constraints they were impotent to alter. This is not to suggest that an observer who visits these classrooms would not be impressed by the teachers and their audience, but rather to emphasize that the teachers knew that what they thought, felt, and did on the stage of their "theater" had in some ways been changed by events offstage.

Just as no one in the conventional performing arts is ever in doubt that his or her performance depends, for good or for bad, on people and events the audience never sees, so is the teacher never in doubt. However, there is one significant difference. The conventional performing artist does not expect to be interrupted while performing by those who are not in the cast. That is not the case with teachers. Years ago at the Yale Psycho-Educational Clinic we did an informal study in several schools to determine the number of times in 1 week that non-teachers appeared in a school with a specific goal in mind (e.g., supervisors, parents, social workers, school psychologists, speech therapists, policemen, etc.). Not all of these people entered classrooms, but in all cases their goals potentially could have an impact on teachers, and at least one quarter of them entered the classroom. (We did not count the number of times messages came over the school intercom, interrupting everything and everyone!) In two ghetto schools there were on average 93 visitors in that week. In three suburban schools the average was 30. As performers, teachers expect interruptions and, more often than not, they do not view them positively. When a child brings home a note asking parents to come see the teacher, the typical parental response is that something is wrong. That is also the response of teachers to interruptions of their performing role. They tend to see those interruptions as invasions into their domain.

What about the school principal who, like the director of a play, orchestrates a cast of characters and activities to achieve what are considered desirable educational outcomes? How might one characterize his or her relationship to and influence on teachers? To the last question the general answer is identical to that for the director-actor relationship: It varies from smooth sailing to subtle warfare, to open, mutual rejection, after which one of them leaves the scene. The principal-teacher relationship is too complex and varied in its sources and effects to be discussed here. But there is one aspect the ramifications of which are profound in several respects. I refer to the fact that the degree to which a teacher regards the principal positively is in part determined by the degree to which the principal does not intrude on the turf of the teacher. To put it baldly, teachers do not want principals *to direct*, to tell them how to teach and how to manage students. Teachers like principals who support and encourage them from a distance, not by being a frequent visitor who seeks in any way to alter the teacher as performer. The principals know this, they have been teachers, and when they become a principal, they know that any intervention in the organization, pedagogy, social psychology of the classroom will not be received warmly. But they did not become principals to play a passive role; they have ideas about what an effective school is like and, therefore, they have the obligation to do justice to those ideas. However, it is generally the case that a principal will not intervene in classroom life unless the issue is so blatant that failure to act is a betrayal of educational and moral standards. It has been pointed out that educational policies—by a principal, superintendent, and board of education—have little impact on classrooms which are the object of those policies (Pauly, 1991). That, as teachers and administrators attest, is largely due to the fact that when teachers at the beginning of the school day close the doors of their classrooms, their performing role combines executive, legislative, and judicial functions; the teacher is relatively and surprisingly free to interpret, accept, or reject a policy; the teacher is an adult *alone* on the classroom stage. That, I should hasten to add, is true at all levels of education, including colleges and universities. Student audiences aside, teaching is not a public affair.

"Teaching is a lonely profession"—that is the title of a chapter written by Dr. Murray Levine in a book several of us at the Yale Psycho-Educational Clinic wrote in 1966 (Sarason, Levine, Goldenberg, Cherlin, & Bennett, 1966). Of all the chapters in that book, that was the one about which we received the largest number of unsolicited approving letters from teachers. As one teacher put it, "Finally, someone recognizes that although we spend the day with students, as an adult we feel alone in the world, especially those of us who are expected to eat our lunch with the kids." That theme has two significances. The first is that unlike those in other performing arts which require (demand) finely tuned, interconnectedness among all those on the stage, the social-political organization of the school is one in which such face-to-face interconnectedness is absent or minimal. Each teacher is, so to speak, a law unto him or herself. Not only does the teacher look askance at a principal who seeks to change his or her pedagogy and style but also at other teachers who articulate or imply something critical. In other performing arts it is a glimpse of the obvious to the student in training that one is part of a mutuality among the members of the group that exercises restraint over the tendency to do things in one's own way. In the case of teachers, preparatory programs have as one of their "of course" goals to prepare a sole performer, someone who will discharge responsibilities independently. It is as if these preparatory programs say, "Yes, you will be part of a social organization that has purposes, rules, regulations, but you will decide for yourself how best to interpret and implement them." It is, therefore, not surprising that the neophyte teacher approaches the opening of school with a good deal of anxiety about being able effectively to act and be independent; to hide anxieties and "mistakes" from other teachers. The neophyte both fears and treasures independence and isolation; over time, the safety of independence and isolation swamps the strength of the fears.

If anything is incontrovertible in the literature on educational reform, it is how difficult it is to get teachers to change their accustomed beliefs and practices. (That is true of others in the educational hierarchy, but let us stay with teachers.) Their resistance to change should occasion no surprise. None of us likes to change. All of us in the face of change find that we like our "symptoms," that the pain associated with change appears greater than the pain the symptoms engender. But in the case of educational reform the stimulus for change comes far less from teachers than from "higher-ups" or other external forces, and teachers regard that pressure as an unwarranted criticism of what they have been doing. In some reform efforts the aim is to increase the strength and the ways in which teachers as a group can assume new responsibilities, an aim as difficult to achieve as it is laudable. Indeed, some teachers look favorably on such a goal not only as an escape from an unwanted privacy but as a recognition of respect for what teachers can and should do. Sometimes that alteration goes relatively smoothly, but more often it engenders such differences in opinion, arouses heretofore unverbalized interpersonal rivalries, and puts such demands on available time as to cause some teachers to opt out or to drastically limit the achievement of the goals of the reform. Someone has said that the life of an educational reform effort is no more than 5 years, which is another way of saying that the death rattle was audible long before final death. Preparatory programs in no way expose their students to the opportunities, dilemmas, and frustrations of group living in a school, especially when the school is being pressured to change.

Those who are in the conventional performing arts have two types of motivations. The first is that they know they have a personal obligation to develop their craft. They know they are expected to do that. One can put it this way: They are motivated to learn more and to change; they do not want to feel or be perceived as one-dimensional. In part that motivation is built-in because the directors of artistic productions exert such pressure; they are not content merely to accept what the artist does, their self-interest demands that they help the artist develop and change. Both in opera and the theater, artists, even well-known ones, seek coaches who serve as supportive critics and teachers. And in all instances performing artists, especially those of neophyte status, carefully and eagerly observe and learn from more experienced performers with whom they are working.

The second motivation, related to the first, is that the performing artist seeks diversity in role and repertoire. No actor wants to be typecast, as in the case of Luigi Antonelli whom I discussed in Chapter 2. No opera singer wants to sing only Verdi, or Wagner, or Puccini. No pianist wants to be known as competent only to play Mozart or Beethoven, or Chopin. No dancer wants to perform only in the ballets of Balanchine, Graham, or Ashton. The performing artist seeks the challenge of diversity. We are used to hearing that when asked why he seeks to scale Mt. Everest, the mountain climber's answer is, "Because it is there." In each of the performing arts there are Mt. Everests where the danger is not injury or death but the possibility that the artist will not do justice to the role.

It is radically different with teachers. The classroom is the domain they rule, but the ruler is *alone*. They do not seek to invite others into the classroom to be observed, advised, or criticized. They do not ask to observe other teachers. There is little or no professional collegiality if by that you mean a serious discussion of the pedagogical issues and problems teachers confront. There are in some schools "inservice" staff development days when some external expert talks about his or her expertise. With rare exceptions teachers regard these one-shot sessions as uninteresting and unrelated to their daily practice. In many states teachers are required to take some graduate courses to maintain their certification and receive a modest salary increase. Teachers find these courses little more interesting than inservice days.

There is little or nothing in the organization and culture of schools that spurs a teacher to regard change and development as necessary, personally and intellectually rewarding, and *safe*. I emphasize safe because in the culture of the school the teacher who seeks help or coaching from others is one whose competence is called into question. The teacher is expected to handle all problems that arise in the classroom, and it is a sign of weakness if it becomes apparent that that is not the case. No teacher will deny that the beginning teacher is one plagued by anxiety, self-doubt, and fear of exposure. In all my experience over the decades I never knew of a school that made it easy and safe for the beginning teacher to admit some inadequacy and ask for help. This is not to say that experienced teachers are unsympathetic to the neophyte, but rather that they assume offers of help may add to the neophyte's sense of incompetency; besides, it is the rare neophyte who will ask for help. I should emphasize that the school day is not organized to make visitations possible, let alone easy.

What happens over time to teachers when year in and year out they teach the same thing to the same kinds of audiences? What are the sources, internal and external, to give them the sense of growth, to cause them willingly to enlarge or alter their role and repertoire, to prevent the feeling that they have settled into a safe, comfortable routine? The answer is: precious little. The absence of anything resembling professional collegiality, the lack of motivation to read the professional literature (Sarason, 1993c), the adversarial strains and tensions in the school culture between teachers and the administrative hierarchy, the sense of aloneness in a densely populated setting—these are some of the factors conducive to the routinization of thought and practice. These problems are especially relevant to teachers in urban schools where educators are under constant pressure to improve student performance, pressure which has not been successful. In these schools routinization of thought and practice is a process that over time interacts with the equally insidious process of teacher burnout in which teachers conclude that the time, energy, and commitment they give to their students are grossly disproportionate to student outcomes. In Chapter 5 I presented the work and conclusions of Arthur Jersild (1955) who without using the term *burnout* described the sources and consequences of burnout. That was in the 1950s. Beginning in the 1960s professional burnout became a "hot" topic generally and among teachers in particular. That was the decade in which every major societal institution was subject to critical scrutiny and pressure to change, and schools were not exempt. By the end of that decade, and continuing thereafter, a significant number of teachers and administrators left the field or looked forward to early retirement. The explanation is by no means a simple one, but part of that explanation was an unwillingness or inability to adapt to changing times, attitudes, and roles, an adaptation made difficult or impossible by a school culture which never contained or supported the conditions which make professional growth and change safe and desirable. On the contrary, it was a culture which reinforced routinization of thought and practice, as well as narrowness of role.

In all my writing about schools and their personnel I have emphasized what I consider to be a glimpse of the obvious: If the conditions for productive learning do not exist for teachers, they cannot create and *sustain* those conditions for students. So, if you ask college and university faculty to justify the existence of these institutions, the common thread in their answers is that they exist in order to create the conditions in which faculty learn, explore, change, and "grow." When you ask educators to justify the existence of schools, the answer is that they exist for students, period. No two explanations can be more different from each other. What would be surprising is if teachers generally (there are always exceptions) experienced over time the sense of learning, exploring, changing. In the conventional performing arts performers seek novelty and challenge. *They are expected to seek them.* It occasions no surprise when a leading actor in the theater signs a contract not for the entire run of the play, but for a specified number of months; he or she wants and needs new challenges, not satisfied to remain within the confines of challenges met and overcome. There are new worlds to conquer! I have met very, very few teachers who view their futures in that way. Whether they are justified or not, after 5 years in the classroom teachers (again generally speaking) feel they have met the challenge and envision a future as a carbon copy of the present, unaware of the dangers of routinization of thought and practice.

In 1996 I attended in Germany an international conference on teacher burnout. Although my perspective on schools and teaching should not have allowed me to assume that teacher burnout was more serious and frequent in the United States than in countries with very different cultures and systems of education, I was not prepared to learn that it was no less serious and frequent elsewhere. Indeed, in some countries which unlike in the United States have highly centralized, bureaucratically layered and controlled school systems, teacher burnout was reported as no less a problem than in our country. And in all countries dissatisfaction by the public with their schools was loud and getting clearer. Although it was recognized that directing criticism to teachers was an instance of blaming the victim, there was relatively little discussion about what changes would be required to transform schools and preparatory programs so as to make teachers more motivated to enlarge their understanding of themselves and their audiences.

Why are we witness today to calls for smaller class size, preferably 20 or less students? The usual and seemingly obvious answer is that the smaller the class size the more individual attention can be given a student by the teacher. I say that as an act of faith or hope because I have several nagging reservations which prevent me from jumping on the bandwagon, although if I had to vote yes or no, I would certainly vote yes (if only because hope springs eternal). The first reason is that I agree with Mencken's caveat that for every complex problem there is a simple answer that is wrong. And we have been discussing a very complex problem! That is not to say that no positive effects will derive from smaller classes, but rather that these effects will be far from robust, far less than is expected. The second reason is that if nothing else changes in the school, why should smaller classes be a preventive against routinization of thought and practice, fear of and resistance to change, the absence of professional collegiality, burnout, fantasies of early retirement, and school systems unable or unwilling to take staff development seriously? Smaller classes are not like the Salk vaccine which alone reduces the chances to near nil that a child will come down with polio. There have been many instances in the theater where selection or changing of the leading actors could not overcome the fact that the play had all of the ballast of a lead balloon.

The third reason, and in an ultimate sense the most important, has to do with the phrase "giving students more individual attention." Unlike other performing arts where the audience is silent and in no overt sense interacts with those onstage, teachers and students do interact in ways very meaningful to both; they are not the interactions of strangers passing in the night, as is so frequently the case in classrooms. What do we mean by "giving more attention"? I assume the reader will agree that phrase means more than determining how well a student comprehends a particular facet of a subject matter. Take the instance where the student comprehends in the way the teacher intended: the student has learned the "correct" answer or performed an arithmetical operation in an appropriate way. Both teacher and student are satisfied, especially the teacher because the student has learned what he or she needed to learn. Does it, should it, be of interest to the teacher that the student's satisfaction derived solely or largely from having pleased the teacher and not because what he or she learned has any personal or utilitarian value, or has any significance beyond that isolated facet? That is to say, is this a student who wants to learn because what he or she has learned has piqued his curiosity, has enlarged his horizons, has changed his conception of the subject matter and himself in small or large ways? Are these questions implied by the phrase "giving more attention," or are they off-limits, an indulgence of the excesses of an impractical idealism? To which I have to reply that one of the justifications for small classes is the recognition that our classrooms, especially but not exclusively in middle and high schools, are populated by a large number of unmotivated, bored, disinterested students many of whom are in suburban schools where they learn what they are "expected" to learn. (The myth that suburban schools contain a large number of students who enjoy learning to learn and think is not one their teachers believe, test scores to the contrary not withstanding.)

There is an asymmetry in the phrase "giving more attention" in that it engenders imagery of an active teacher and a passive student, a kind of one-way street for giving. The fact is that a student gives far more attention to the teacher—the sole adult agent of authority and fate in the classroom—than the teacher gives to individual students. In general, students may wonder, what does the teacher say or do and why, what pleases or displeases the teacher, why does the teacher call on some children more than on others, why does the teacher laugh so much or so little, why does the teacher seem to like some students more than others, is the teacher married and does he or she have children, what does the teacher do outside of school? There are other questions more personally important to a student: Does the teacher really like me? Does she really have an idea about what I feel and what I think about? Is he interested in me? Can it be that she thinks she knows me? Does he want to know what I do at home, where I go, my hobbies, what turns me on and what turns me off? When I don't understand something she is teaching or showing me, why am I afraid to tell her? Surface appearances aside, "students give attention" to the teacher, but they have many questions, most of which never get asked. In fact, students ask *subject matter*, not personal questions, at a level not much above zero (Susskind, 1969/1970). In that research personal questions were not recorded because, for all practical purposes, they are zero. Although there are the usual exceptions, the interactions between student and teacher are superficial, or shallow, or very transient.

In the musical *The King and I* the new British teacher introduces herself to the Siam king's children (approximately 20!) by singing the song, "Getting to Know You." The point of the song, of course, is that if the children are to learn from her she must by words and action convince them that she truly wants and has to know and understand them. She is a performing artist whose task it is to enable her audience to regard her as believable, someone with whom they can identify. She knows, as do the children, that she is an adult, not a child; and therein lies the challenge: How does an adult have to perform so that she not only feels secure that she knows and understands the learner but also that the learner is convinced of it? And the payoff is in the reaction of the audience: wanting to learn subject matter, to explore, to be and feel competent. (It is interesting that in *The Sound of Music*, by Rogers and Hammerstein, the same theme-rationale is present. And, more recently, the film *Mr. Holland's Opus* makes all the points I have tried to make. You cannot understand these points by my words or those of others, except in a vague, impersonal way. It is when you can observe these points in action and connect them with personal history and experience that these points take on concrete, compelling meaning. Words have their place and value, but we must never confuse words with the things, events, or transactions they signify.)

Some people may argue that I am asking too much of teachers, that it is too much to expect that they possess the knowledge and competency to perform in ways I have suggested, that I am asking them to be both accomplished performer and astute psychologist. My answer is in several parts. First, I have observed teachers of 25 or more students who handled some (not all) students in accord with what I have indicated (which was indicated by others long before I entered the educational scene; nothing I have said is new). The number of such teachers is few, dramatically less than the number of teachers like Mr. Holland was before he realized why he had been a total failure as a teacher. Second, what I am asking of teachers is not on a par with quantum mechanics or relativity theory for strangeness or unfamiliarity. It is not an arcane mystery. I shall have more to say about this shortly. The third part of my answer is that I expect, and I would hope others would expect, that when we hear that reducing class size is for the purpose of allowing teachers to take the individuality of children seriously that it means that the style, substance, and course of the teacher-student relationship will literally look and be different than it looks now. Or is "giving more individual attention" a slogan, a buzz word, a legitimization of more of the same, a badge of virtue empty of meaning? What is meant when we are piously told that we owe it to each student to help him or her to realize his or her potential? Can that even be approximated by doing more of the same? And do we mean that lofty goal to include all students: those who will go to college, those who will enter the work force, those who are intellectually handicapped? Nothing in what I have said should be interpreted as referring only, or even predominantly, to college-bound students. When I say "subject matter" I mean the formal intellectual-conceptual content, call it for convenience "the curriculum," considered realistically necessary to master if the student is to stand a chance to achieve whatever life goals the student envisions. It should make no difference whatever program, stream, or school a student is in; the obligation of the teacher to that student is the same as for any other category of student. Subject matter is crucially of bedrock importance, so important that it cannot be allowed to be taught in ways as to cause students to regard it as an empty exercise isolated from their unarticulated thoughts, feelings, questions, and goals. Subject matter is not something that should remain "outside" but rather something that is absorbed in the psychological bloodstream and has internal propelling consequences. I am not an advocate of a "touchy-feely" pedagogy. I am an advocate of a pedagogy that weds subject matter with a student's way of seeing and experiencing self and his or her surrounding world.

Having said all of the above, I have to say that I agree that my expectations of teachers are unrealistic, if by unrealistic is meant that the selection and preparation of teachers have been and still are so grossly inadequate and misguided as to put my expectations in the realm of fantasy. The major implication of what I have said and will say is that the selection and preparation of teachers are in need of a radical overhaul. I do not kid myself that this implication will sit well in many quarters either because of vested interests or because some know that the fruits of such a radical overhaul will take years to be implemented before its effects will be apparent. Those who want "solutions" now, or in the foreseeable future, who put their hopes on simple solutions (like class size), who cannot confront or explain why the educational reform movement in the post World War II era has so little to show are allowing their understandable and even laudable hopes to cause them to tinker on the edges of a very complicated, disturbing set of issues.

In Chapters 8 and 9 I will deal with the issues of the selection and preparation of teachers. But before doing so, the next chapter is taken from *The Making of an American Psychologist* (1989), my autobiography which was written a decade ago. I include this chapter because it will allow me in a concrete, personal way to begin to put some flesh on the bones of abstractions. The central character is a teacher, Henry Schaefer-Simmern, whom I met shortly after I took my first professional job in 1942 at the Southbury Training School in Connecticut, a brand new state institution. He forever changed my life as well as the lives of some of the residents. He was the quintessential performing artist. But only when he was with his students!

CHAPTER 7

Discovering the Significance of Art for Psychology and Education

I called him Schaefer, he called me Seymour. When we met at Southbury in 1943, I was 24; he was 45. I was American; he was a political refugee from Hitler Germany, having come here several years before. I was a psychologist; he had been a professor of art history and art education in Frankfurt. He lived in Manhattan. He had received a special fellowship from the Russell Sage Foundation to pursue his studies of artistic activity. He was visiting Southbury to determine whether it would be possible and feasible to conduct studies with mentally retarded individuals. That was what Mr. Roselle told me about Henry Schaefer-Simmern before I met him. Typically, Mr. Roselle was proud that Russell Sage had asked him to consider providing "the Professor" with a studio where he and his students could work. Mr. Roselle had already decided where the studio would be and what other material resources would be provided. My job would be to help select the kind of resident Schaefer considered appropriate to his goals and to be as helpful as I could be in making his stay at Southbury productive for him and us. He would be coming up for 2 or 3 days each week. A small apartment would be provided him.

Schaefer was a tall, large man with piercing eyes in a serious face. His English was comprehensible, but with a decided German accent. Initially, he struck me as fitting my stereotype of a Prussian: deadly serious, rigid, authoritarian, forceful, opinionated. I had never met a *political* refugee from Hitler Germany. And here was one who struck me as "typically" German, the kind of person who made Hitler possible. It was not a difficult first meeting. We were both polite, obviously feeling each other out. How could I be helpful to him, I asked. He answered by attempting to explain his "theory" of artistic development and activity. It was hard for me to follow him, but two things were clear in what he said: artistic activity was a normal attribute of *all* people, and it was an attribute that the educational system and the culture of which it was a part effectively extinguished with its misguided belief that art was (had to be) the copying of reality. Schaefer's life goal had been and would continue to be to demonstrate the validity of his theory with individuals who were considered uncreative or considered themselves uncreative. He had worked with workers and institutionalized delinquents, among other groups. He had never worked with mentally retarded individuals, and that is why he was at Southbury. What he wanted from me was a list of residents with whom I thought he could work. We would then call each to my office and Schaefer would talk with them and ask them to draw anything they wanted, on the basis of which Schaefer would make his selection. I said I would prepare the list and he could begin to see each of these residents the following week when he would begin his 2- or 3-day visits to Southbury. What he was after and how to prepare such a list mystified me. Were this man and his mission going to be an ongoing, unsought burden?

That first meeting had consequences for me. One was the memory it engendered of a traumatic event I had experienced in the third or fourth grade. It was during a class conducted by a "drawing" teacher. She came into the room with a coffee percolator, passed out paper, and told us to draw the percolator. I remember asking myself, why are we being asked to draw the percolator? I tried, oh did I try, to draw that damned percolator, but only by the wildest stretches of the imagination did it remotely look like the percolator. I looked around me and saw that the other children were drawing percolators that looked a little like Mrs. Pearson's percolator. Why couldn't I do it? Which is exactly the question Mrs. Pearson asked me. Psychologically I began to shrivel up, I was flooded with anxiety, and I wanted to cry. Was this what Schaefer was talking about when he said that requiring children to copy reality doomed them to failure and to regard themselves as devoid of artistic ability? Was this what he meant when he said that even if the artist wants to, he or she cannot duplicate reality because reality is too complex? Was I not one of those people socialized to believe that artistic ability was a special ability that the fates obviously had denied me? Schaefer became more interesting to me.

The second consequence was the realization that for all practical purposes I knew nothing about art. I knew the names of the great artists. I had gone to see the Van Gogh exhibit because it was an event, a happening, going to which testified to one's respect for "culture." In that first meeting, Schaefer had referred to several artists as if I knew who they were, and he had also emphasized that what he stood for was a direct continuation of the ideas of Gustave Britsch, Conrad Fiedler, and several others, all of whom were well-known figures in the field of theories of art and utterly unknown to me. Schaefer had also told me that he had the highest respect for John Dewey's understanding of the nature and significance of artistic activity. I did not know very much about Dewey except that he was identified with three fields: psychology long ago, philosophy, and education. Schaefer must have sensed my puzzlement about Dewey in relation to art, because he said that Dewey's book *Art as Experience* (1934) was a twentieth-century classic that I *must* read. (Schaefer was incapable of making a suggestion with neutral affect.)

The third was less a consequence in the narrow sense than a vague intuition that I was not in the same league with him, that he was a man of vast erudition capable of high-order conceptualizing and theorizing, that in any relationship with him I would be a student and probably not a good one. That in no way lessened my own sense of worth. I felt that I had met a man who lived and pushed the intellectual life to its limits, and I envied him.

Before going on with the development of our relationship, one that terminated with his death several years ago at age 81, let me relate what happened at the second meeting when I lined up a dozen or so residents for him to see. I have no clear memory of how I had selected them. All but three were female. Two of the males were known in the institution for their unusual interest in drawing and ability to draw. Their ages ranged from 20 to 40. Their IQs ranged from 40 to 80. Their formal diagnosis was familial retardation, variously called subcultural, garden-variety, or Kallikak mental retardation. One of them, who plays an important role in this story, was also psychotic, but not obviously so. Why I included her I cannot remember. They had been at Southbury, or the older institution at Mansfield, from a minimum of 3 to a maximum of 20 years.

I brought each resident in and introduced him or her to Schaefer. They sat at my desk, and I sat a couple of feet away and could observe both of them. On the basis of my impression of Schaefer from the first meeting, I was fearful that his imposing bulk would intimidate the residents, that his German accent would not be intelligible to them, and that his serious, forbidding manner would be an obstacle to rapport. I watched him with that first resident, and I was flabbergasted. It was as if his entire musculature relaxed, his voice lowered and softened, and he looked at and spoke to the resident with *respect*. I do not know how else to put it. It was not only that he showed interest but that he regarded the resident with a mixture of curiosity, tenderness, and importance. He did not smile, he was always task oriented, and he was always accepting. Do you like to draw, paint, color? What do you like to draw? He gently asked these and related questions, and then he gave them a sheet of paper and requested that they draw whatever they wanted. When they were through, he looked with great interest at what they had drawn. Several questions might follow. Do you like what you have done? Would you like to try to do it again or draw something else? Is there anything about the drawing you do not like? That you would like to change? He spent at least 15 minutes with each resident.

During it all, I kept wondering on what basis he would select residents for his "studio." Would he choose Rudy, whose florid, semi-chaotic drawings had such graceful, flowing lines? Would he choose Selma, who drew stick figures, and very simple ones? Within one minute after the last resident left, Schaefer told me which six he had chosen. How did you choose, I asked him? He divided the drawings into two groups, spreading them out in a way as to make comparisons possible.

It did not require study to conclude that there was an obvious difference. The drawings of the residents who were not selected were, relatively speaking, complicated in a busy way, with overlapping lines, figures, and objects. The drawings of the selected residents could be called primitive, Selma's stick figures being an example. To me, the drawings of the unselected residents were more "artistic." I asked Schaefer why he made the choices he did. His answer remains vivid in my mind. It is not a verbatim quotation, I am sure, but the italicized words or sentences reflect his emphasis. In an intellectual discussion, Schaefer rarely uttered a sentence that did not contain at least one word to which he gave special emphasis. "These [referring to unselected residents] are drawings from *memory*. They tried to imitate *reality*. And the more they tried to do the *impossible—no* artist, *not even da Vinci*, can *copy* reality in all its details—the more the visual chaos. They did not draw according to an inner process of *visual conceiving* but according to their cognitions about reality, and, therefore, it is a memory game. Their artistic development has been *spoiled*. They tried to do something far beyond their level of visual conceiving. These [referring to the selected residents] are not yet *spoiled*. They drew what *they* can *see* in accordance with their level of visual conceiving. They did not *intend* to copy reality. To *you* it is primitive: there are no overlapping lines, each figure stands by itself, each figure is made up of circles and horizontal and vertical lines, you *cannot change the direction of any one line without changing the other lines*. Primitive, *yes*, but in accordance with *their* level of visual conceiving, their level of *gestalt formation*. They see on the paper what they *can* see, not what reality says they *should* see. They are not yet *spoiled*. They can develop. I shall work with them."

I felt that what he said was terribly important, but I could hardly digest it. During the next few days, I found myself obsessively returning to what he had said. I replayed again and again my experience with having to draw the percolator. Could there be any doubt that what he had said explained in large part my inability to meet the requirements of copying reality, that trying to represent the curvatures of the percolator was way beyond whatever Schaefer meant by my level of visual conceiving? Was he not right in his view that artistic creativity is a universal human attribute that gets extinguished in most of us because we are unable to meet external criteria discrepant with our level of development, what he called our stage of development of visual conceiving? Was not his emphasis on the gestalt qualities of an artistic effort—that the integrity of the forms on the paper are reflective of an internal conceptual integrity—completely consistent with what I knew from the writings of the Gestalt psychologists such as Wertheimer, Koffka, Kohler?

About one thing I was crystal clear: Schaefer, like me, held the Rousseau-like view that our culture in general, and our educational institutions in particular, do an effective job in masking human potential. Unlike me, Schaefer held that view in relation to a specific type of human activity for which he was formulating a stage-developmental theory based on longitudinal studies of individuals. (There is more to it than individual studies, but that comes later.) Like me, Schaefer came to Southbury to demonstrate that *"even* mentally retarded people are capable of more than we think."

But there was another thing about those first two meetings that bothered and stirred me. Why was my education so utterly devoid of exposure to the world of art? And in education I include my graduate training in psychology. Not only had I never been exposed to psychology in relation to art, but I could not remember any seminar in which the nature of creativity had been discussed. I knew and used Goodenough's Draw-A-Man test, but that was an *intelligence* test. If Schaefer was right, as intuitively I felt he was, psychologists, like everyone else, believed that art required a special ability. You either had it or you didn't. And precisely because it was a special and infrequent ability, why should it be in the mainstream of the field? If someone had a special interest in a special ability, then he or she should pursue that interest, but that was no warrant for saying that it should be of general interest to psychology, or for it occupying time in the education of psychologists. And here was Schaefer insisting that artistic ability was universal and contained keys to understanding the nature and vicissitudes of human creativity!

Following the second meeting in my office—he was at Southbury for 3 days—I sought him out and plied him with questions. It was the beginning of a father-son, teacher-student, friend relationship. I did not know it then, but Schaefer was a lonely man. It was not only that his ideas ran counter to conventional wisdom. He was not an easy person to be with. That was the judgment of most people. Our 40-year relationship was a personal and intellectual delight. He was a man of single purpose: his work and his ideas were his life. He would talk about these matters with passion. Little else interested him. To say that he did not suffer fools gladly is truly an extreme form of understatement. He was not an ogre. He was not a hostile person. He was incapable of small talk. If you treated him with respect, he would be polite and gracious even if inside he had disdain for you. Schaefer was an elitist, and in a strange way. He felt comfortable with "ordinary" people who did not pretend to be intellectuals. In his words, they were not "spoiled." But God help you if you were an inhabitant of the intellectual world and, in Schaefer's view, a superficial thinker, a dilettante, a self-aggrandizing entrepreneur, a status-seeking climber, singly or in any combination. His disdain could be of majestic proportions, although he usually hid it and would avoid these people like the plague. His experience in and around academia produced few people he could respect. Few people met his standards either of intellectual seriousness or of personal conduct. If he cottoned to me, it was because it was obvious that I was interested in his ideas and work, respected him, was willing to be helpful, and put right out on the table that in matters of art I was an ignoramus who wanted to learn. I was and am no shrinking violet, and I could challenge and argue with him about anything without arousing the slightest sense of pique. We never articulated what was obvious. We loved each other.

As a result of my questions, Schaefer brought up the following week a series of "cases," each of which contained the artistic development of individuals none of whom ever considered themselves artists. Two were unforgettable. Indeed, my initial reaction was one of disbelief. When you looked at their first and their latest efforts, it was the difference between crawling and running, between knowing that one and one are two and being able to solve a quadratic equation. In all of the cases, the initial productions were simple and ordered, possessing gestalt qualities, but in no way impressive to a viewer. As you went from one drawing to another, you could see slight but increasing differentiation and complexity. By the time you reached their latest drawings or paintings or sculptures, you would have visions of delight at the prospect of having them on display in your home. But during and after viewing the several cases, I had a sinking sensation around the troubling thought that this single-minded, obsessed, intellectual missionary was totally unaware that he had instructed these individuals how to do or improve their drawings. My training as a psychologist may have been incomplete or deficient in a number of respects but not in regard to how easy it is for our passionately held ideas and values to influence and direct the behavior of others, especially in relationships of unequal power and status. If that was the case with Schaefer, it was also the case that I could not discuss it with him. I had better, I thought, tread very lightly. And, yet, there was a part of me that wanted (indeed, needed) to believe that he was right.

It is not a digression here to discuss Carl Rogers's *Counseling and Psychotherapy* (1942), which was published the year before Schaefer came to Southbury. It is hard to exaggerate the impact of that book on me particularly and psychology generally. For one thing, here was a psychologist writing about psychotherapy; that is, presenting his therapeutic work and offering a very distinctive conceptualization that determined his technique. Nondirective psychotherapy did not *impose* restrictions on the therapist but rather enabled him or her to be exquisitely sensitive to what a client was saying in the here and now. Personal history, the results of diagnostic testing, unconscious meanings, and the like had relevance only insofar as they were contained in what the client *said* he or she was thinking and feeling *at the moment* in the relationship. The task of the therapist was to state or restate what the client said, as if one were holding up an auditory "mirror" for the client to see himself or herself, to examine and re-examine what they had said about themselves. And, Rogers argued and his cases indicated, that process of examination and re-examination enabled the client to clarify and reformulate perception of self and problem. The client possessed the seeds of change and growth; the nondirective technique enabled the client to see and nurture those seeds. The therapist did not direct or interpret but rather stated or restated the client's communication as if to say, "Is this what you are saying? Is this what you mean for me to understand?" So, to a client who says that he or she feels unloved, Rogers might say, "Are you saying that *no one* on this earth loves or has affection for you?" To which the client would likely say, "Oh, no, there are people who love me, like *A* or *B* or *C*. What I meant was. . . ."

That a psychologist was doing, theorizing about, and writing about psychotherapy in 1942 was startling in itself. But no less startling, truly revolutionary, was that he presented verbatim transcripts of the therapy. I said earlier that Rogers's book had impact on me and on psychology. That is a misleading judgment, because his use and publication of verbatim transcripts threw down the gauntlet to the entire mental health community, especially psychiatry to, so to speak, put up or shut up. It is as if Rogers was saying, "We have had a surfeit of theorizing, anecdotal evidence, case summarizing in regard to what we do and why in psychotherapy. What we have lacked are the raw data by which to judge the relationship among theory, technique, and outcome. In this book you have the raw data by which to judge my ideas, technique, and success." And the outcomes were impressive.

Just as I was not disposed to accept Schaefer's explanation of the work of his students, I could not dispute his "raw data"; just as the reader could not dispute the validity of Rogers's transcripts, the mental health community was not disposed to accept Rogers's explanation of outcomes. The question that was raised most frequently and cogently was, how nondirective was Rogers? People pored over those transcripts searching for evidence that Rogers was not as nondirective as he said he was or his theory required. My own assessment at the time, not different from that of others, was that Rogers fell short of perfection but that he had a very high batting average. I reached that conclusion reluctantly, because nondirective therapy was so different from the psychoanalytical approaches to which I was very partisan.

All of this was buzzing around in my head during those early weeks with Schaefer. Was Schaefer as nondirective as he claimed? Was there not some kind of implicit affinity between Rogers's belief in a client's capacity to see and alter perceptions without substantive direction from the therapist, and Schaefer's insistence that the "unfolding" of artistic activity would be manifested if, and only if, you enabled the person to build on his or her level of visual conceiving uninfluenced by external criteria of how one should draw? And even if Schaefer and Rogers were correct in their explanations, how much of the outcomes they reported was due to the kinds of persons they were? There is theory and there is technique, but there is also a human being in whom they are supposed to be appropriately integrated. And if we know anything about that integration, it is how dramatically different it looks in different people. From my observations of Schaefer with residents in my office, I knew he was capable of being with them in a warm, sensitive, and dispassionate way. Those observations were indeed compelling, contrasting as they did with his usual manner.

What came to mind was an experience I had at Clark University observing Charlotte Bühler with a young child through a one-way screen. In 1939–40, Charlotte and Karl Bühler were at Clark for the year as visiting professors. Karl had been one of the greats in European psychology. He was known in America, but to a far lesser extent than Charlotte because many of his works were untranslated. When he came to this country (he was not Jewish, Charlotte was), he was a defeated, depressed man but quintessentially the responsive gentleman. Charlotte, who had been one of his students, had a deserved international reputation in child development. And Charlotte not only considered herself a queen, but she acted and dressed accordingly. She was seen by students as fascinating, arrogant, cold, and impossible. On the first day of her seminar, she began by telling us of a meeting "at which I took place." She then asked us whether we had heard about or read anything of Freud. Midway into the seminar, she said that she wanted us to observe her with a child. *That* we had to see! It was inconceivable to us that she could do other to the girl than intimidate and scare her. We were flabbergasted by what we saw and heard. Neither before nor since have I seen anyone more comforting and sensitive with a preschooler, or elicit in a more nondirective way what interested the child; that is, follow where the child psychologically was and wanted to go. If she was directive, it escaped us. If we had a videotape of that session, I am sure one could find elements of directiveness, as in the case of Rogers. But those elements would not obscure her "ability" to build on what was in the mind of the child, to bring to configurated expression what was inside that young girl's head.

How did Schaefer get his students to develop artistically as his longitudinal case material demonstrated? How consistent was he with his view that every "unspoiled" person was capable of a stage-like development, each stage of which had its own visual-conceptual, gestalt properties that could not and should not be hurried or bypassed? Did he really enable or empower that process without "teaching" them, without telling them what and how to draw? I wanted very much to believe that Schaefer was correct, because it would confirm my conviction that we vastly underestimate human abilities, their nature, variety, and vicissitudes. But when I looked at those longitudinal case studies of "ordinary people," I had to be skeptical. And he was proposing to demonstrate his view by working with institutionalized mentally retarded people! There was a part of me that said, a likely story!

I spent a lot of time in that studio at Southbury. Schaefer met with his students two or three consecutive mornings a week. Over a 2-year period, he started and ended with the same residents, probably six to eight in number. When you walked into the studio, you would be struck by the fact that each student was working in the most concentrated way on his or her drawing—not for 5 or 10 minutes but over long periods of time. They might stop and *study* what they had done, add a line or figure, or take another piece of paper and start over. They might get up and converse with someone else about what they were doing, why, and the problem they were having. If you observed what each student was doing, you would have to note that no two students were drawing the same thing in terms of content, color, and complexity. You would label each of them as simple or primitive by the same criteria by which you would label a Grandma Moses painting; that is, there were no overlapping lines (early in their development), each figure or object was distinct, and the whole thing added up to a gestalt so that *if you changed the direction of one line, or changed a color, you would have to change almost everything else in the work.* You would also note that Schaefer sat at his desk working, usually writing. His interactions with the students were *always* dyadic. He never, but never, addressed them as a class. One of them might walk to his desk and show him what she had just completed. He would study it in the most interested, serious way. Early in the game, the student might ask him: "Do you like this?" And his set response was, "The important thing is whether you like it. Is there anything about it you would like to change or add? You are doing fine. If you started again, would you do it the same way? *Do you see what you want to see?"* That last question was, it turned out, crucial, because it required the student to reflect and study the work, and, far more often than not, it elicited some kind of dissatisfaction with this or that aspect, or a suggestion from the student as to what the next effort would be. Several times a student said, for example, that the tree he or she had drawn did not look like a "real" tree. To which Schaefer would respond with supportive emphasis: "No one can draw a real tree. There are too many branches, too many leaves. That is impossible. You have to draw it so that you see *what you* want to see." Schaefer was certainly directive when he would tell the students that trying to copy reality would get them into "visual" trouble—as he would say to me, "That leads to mental confusion and chaos, and the person gives up or draws an abstraction, not a visual conception." But that kind of direction was for the explicit purpose of reinforcing self-direction. Schaefer was able to get the students not to ignore reality but to transform it in ways satisfactory to the eye, what he called a visual conception, a configurated unity, however simple. He got them to study and reflect, happily to struggle and persevere, to a degree that was utterly unpredictable from their case histories and test results.

There were times when he would study a work and say, pointing to a particular part of it, "Were you having trouble here?" Or he might say about that part, "How do you feel about that?" And there were times when he would say to a student dissatisfied with what she had done, "Maybe if you took a larger piece of paper and worked with crayons, you might like it better."

The point of all this is that Schaefer intruded minimally into a student's development. And he was patient. Over a period of weeks, a student might have made a couple of dozen or more drawings with no two being the same. On quick glance, drawing B would look like drawing A, but, as Schaefer would show me, there was always something different. Drawing C would look like B, but again there was some kind of difference. It was only when you compared A with Z that you immediately saw development, a discernible change in visual clarity and gestalt qualities. He never hurried the students. He accepted and respected what they did. He treated them as if they were serious artists, and to Schaefer they were. "What their work has in common with that of da Vinci is the ordered, configurated, gestalt qualities of their artistic expression. They are, of course, at different stages, but that is no reason for overlooking that their work reflects an artistic process of visual conceiving and expression, a universal process and attribute."

There is a problem, this one between me and the reader. It is unsolvable if you mean by *solvable* that four divided by two is two. At best, lan-

guage can give you a slight idea of a visual work of art. At worst, it conjures up imagery dramatically different from what the work looks like to
the eye. Language may be the best means of communication we have, but
as a way of describing art it is very imperfect. I have expressed my surprise and skepticism at what Schaefer had shown me about his previous
students and what he proposed to demonstrate at Southbury. I assume that
in reading this account the reader has felt frustrated at not being able to
see what my words have tried to suggest. It would be strange if the reader
felt otherwise. Shortly before Schaefer came to Southbury, he had begun
writing a book. His felicity in writing English was barely fair. He was aware
of this as he was of the inherent impossibility of using language to describe
art. Schaefer accepted my offer to edit the chapters sentence by sentence.
We would sit for hours, both of us struggling to make the text illuminate a
drawing, to explain the drawing in terms of Schaefer's theory of stages of
artistic development. Fortunately, his writing got clearer as he got into the
book, reducing somewhat the frustration of finding the right words for what
he wanted to say.

The book was finished after I left Southbury and Schaefer went to
the University of California at Berkeley. It was published in 1948 by that
university's press and has gone through numerous printings. The apt title
was *The Unfolding of Artistic Activity*. I entreat the reader to look at and
read that book. One of the last things John Dewey wrote was the preface
to that book. Schaefer had made it his business to meet Dewey, because
he considered Dewey's *Art as Experience* as one of this century's great
books, a judgment with which I concurred after Schaefer insisted I read
the book. Schaefer opened up for me the world of John Dewey, for which
I am eternally grateful.

The employees at all levels of Southbury looked upon Schaefer as a
"character," some suspicious because he was German and others, especially
those in the education department, because they sensed that he took a very
dim view of how the abilities of the residents were regarded and shaped.
To most of them, what Schaefer was doing with his students was a frivo-
lous luxury, a waste of good space, materials, and the residents' time and
energies. After several months, given the finely honed efficiency of an institution gossip mill, word got around that the residents not only were
making some very interesting drawings but were using these drawings to
pattern and make rugs, place mats, and wall hangings. Without question,
Selma was the resident that was most intriguing to the employees. She was
very mentally retarded, introverted in the extreme, and probably schizo-
phrenic to boot. She looked and acted like a cipher; she washed floors,
worked in the hot laundry, and bothered no one. No one had visited her
for years. Her case history contained a litany of every type of child abuse.

Some of the employees had seen her work in the studio (which Schaefer made into a museum), and others began to visit the studio. Schaefer decided to publicly exhibit her work. Her cottage parents agreed to make the cottage into an art gallery for a two-day exhibit over a weekend. What happened over that weekend was what happens when a museum opens a Picasso retrospective, or when the president of the United States opens a world's fair. The crowds descended; there were waiting lines and much talk. What drew the most attention were Selma's rugs made from discarded clothing. More than a few observers would not believe that what they saw were Selma's *creations*. And in the middle of all this was Selma: now beaming, now tearful, now puzzled and overwhelmed by the attention she was receiving.

What Schaefer enabled these residents to accomplish has to be contrasted with another story. After the exhibit, several employees asked Schaefer to "teach" them. He was reluctant to do so, because he assumed that they were already unrescuably "spoiled," that is, that they had overlearned the stance that the task of the artist was to copy reality. He liked the employees who made the request, he took satisfaction from the changed attitudes toward him the requests signified, and he agreed to meet with them two evenings a week. I observed carefully what went on during the initial weeks. I rarely have seen people struggling as hard or experience so much frustration. Not only was what they attempted to do in their initial efforts difficult in terms of composition—far beyond what Schaefer would say was their stage of visual conception—but they could not unimprison themselves from the tendency to judge their efforts by the criterion of external reality. They could not go back to the beginning, to those early stages where what the eye sees is simple and ordered and on the basis of which greater ordered complexity becomes possible. They wanted to run before they could crawl or walk. All but two gave up, but those two "got the message" and showed a startling development—startling to them, not to Schaefer. Those observations seared into my mind the conviction—to me it is an unfortunate, brute fact—that in their emphasis on memory and abstractions, their fantastic underestimation and ignoring of curiosity and creativity, the socialization and education processes obscure human capabilities. But, Schaefer would point out, that is not the case in all societies, present or past. Over the years, Schaefer had collected hundreds, if not thousands, of pictures of art (paintings, sculpture, and so on) from cultures in all parts of the world demonstrating stage-like progressions identical to what you will see in his book. What I learned from Schaefer about human abilities, cognitive development, and our educational theories, practices, and institutions influenced everything I have ever done. It is not happenstance that John Dewey saw fit to write the preface to Schaefer's book.

Dewey, like Schaefer, saw that where you stand on the nature of artistic activity as an instance of creativity is where you stand on the processes and goals of education. There are very few others—frankly, no other names come to mind—who saw and wrote about that connection with the clarity and incisiveness (and implicit despair) of Dewey and Schaefer.

There was one disagreement between Schaefer and me, one of emphasis rather than principle. Schaefer presented his theory of the development of visual conceiving in a way that could give people the impression that the "unfolding" of artistic activity was, so to speak, programmed in the individual, that if you did not interfere in that unfolding, the development would run its natural course. I did not disagree with the thrust of his argument—you could not disagree with the longitudinal "data" he presented—but I felt that he was underplaying the roles of context and meaning. In short, he was underplaying the crucial role he played, past and present, in creating the social context and in acting in ways that enabled or empowered individuals to start and go forward. As with Carl Rogers and Charlotte Bühler, the outcomes of Schaefer's efforts were not independent of what he was as a mentor: the respect he showed his students, the encouragement he gave to them, the patience he had, and, crucially, his sensitivity to the problems a student would encounter within a particular stage and in moving to the next stage (for example, from exclusive use of horizontal and vertical lines to diagonal ones). I was already enough of a clinician to know that whatever the virtues of theory, its operational significance inhered in how it was manifest in practice. However well I understood Schaefer's theory, never in a million years could I even approach doing what he did. What Schaefer had trouble confronting was his ability to create a context that had all of the characteristics that make for productive learning. When I would contrast the behavior of the Southbury residents in Schaefer's studio—truly a group within which each individual was distinctive and of which Schaefer was a member—with what you would see in classrooms in the school at Southbury, it was the difference between night and day. Schaefer, of course, knew this, but he could not bring himself to give it the significance it deserved. His main task in life, he said again and again, was to demonstrate that artistic activity and development were universal human attributes. *That* is what the world needed to know, and *that* was his mission. The emphasis I entreated him to consider would be the task of others, always a few, who would understand what he had done and written. He had to finish the book he was writing, because then he could start on his magnum opus: demonstrating his theory with art in scores of cultures, past and present. That book would take years, he knew. He was well into middle age, he had had a heart attack, time was not on his side. When he died several years ago at age 81, the book was not finished. It took me years to understand that there was a part of him that felt that when he finished that book, his life would be over, his mission completed. It was as if he delayed and delayed its completion as a way of living with the mission, not completing it. Without the mission to keep him going, he would be more alone than he already was. Whenever we got together, in Berkeley or New Haven, I would implore, encourage, beg him to get it done. I had seen the "data" that would be in the book. I knew that he took yearly trips to Germany because there was a company there that could make the reproductions the way he wanted. To say that Schaefer was a perfectionist is a monumental understatement.

No one can understand me as person or professional without knowing my relationship with Schaefer. What I absorbed from him, as I shall shortly elaborate, took place in the best of all contexts in which the intellectual, interpersonal, and social features were indissolubly integrated. Schaefer would often say that I was one of a few people who understood his theory. I could never bring myself to say that that was a misleading judgment, that what I understood was the lack of boundaries among his theory, his practice, and *him*.

What did I get from Schaefer? Let me start with something that was both humbling and unsettling. Schaefer was the first person I knew who had a truly classical education. I once said to a friend, "Why should I buy the *Encyclopedia Britannica*, when I have Schaefer?" His knowledge of languages and world history was staggering. And when I say knowledge, I do not mean facts. It was knowledge organized for his purposes. It was as if all of human experience and knowledge existed for him to use depending on his immediate purpose. Rarely did we have a discussion without his connecting and illustrating it by reference to some past figure, event, or era, with line and verse. For example, I do not remember the specific focus of the conversation, but at one point he said something like this, "That is something Goethe understood and wrote about in his diary of his trip through Italy. He was in Perugia that summer, in July, and. . . ." On another occasion, when we were struggling for the words to describe the problem one of the residents was having in her drawing, Schaefer stopped for a moment as if lost in reflection and then said that what the resident was confronted with was beautifully illustrated in a series of murals painted by an unknown Egyptian artist several thousand years ago during the reign of a pharaoh whose name Schaefer gave, and then he went on to say in which museum it was housed. Philosophy, social history, intellectual history, religious history—it was as if he had it all in his head, productively organized and usable.

What was unsettling about this was not only the fact that I had not had a classical education but the dawning realization that education in

America has severed its roots and connections with what was best in the traditions of classical education. The sense of history and rootedness—that was what had gone by the boards in education in America. Separated from the rest of the world by two vast oceans, we were also separated from our roots, from a sense of continuity. Schaefer understood this, but what he bemoaned most was our ignorance of the fact that the American worldview was incomprehensible without the sense of history and continuity. But there was another source of my unsettlement. If I knew a fraction of what Schaefer knew, I would be a better psychologist. If American psychology grounded itself, as it did and does, in the narrow (relatively speaking) traditions of science, its view of humanity would have all of the deficits of rampant parochialism. A psychology that regarded creativity as a small and narrow tributary of the mainstream of psychology—worthy, of course, of study but not central to understanding human behavior—was an impoverished psychology. What Schaefer drummed into my head was that artistic activity was central for a number of reasons, not the least of which was the way it required us to look at the educational process in our schools. He would become literally livid when he described how our schools extinguished rather than nurtured the unfolding of human capacities. Working, as I was, in an educational institution (for the mentally retarded no less) meant that I was far from the mainstream of American psychology. That didn't bother me. What Schaefer did was to make me proud that I was in an arena of thought and work fateful for a society. Before I met Schaefer, I wanted to save the world. After I met him, I knew that I would do it in the field of education. I was no less grandiose than Schaefer. Our grandiosity was one of the ties that bound us together. If a part of each of us knew how unrealistic we were, we helped each other ignore it.

It was not simply that Schaefer had a classical education but that he milked it. From the time I met Schaefer, especially after I left Southbury and came to Yale in 1945, the substance and goals of education in America became a dominating interest in my life, but not without its problems. On the one hand, if I pursued that interest, I would have to not only re-educate myself but also forego a career in an academic psychology that regarded the field of education with at best disinterest and at worst derogation. On the other hand, I did have strong interests in problems that were more attuned to the zeitgeist in psychology that I wanted to pursue. The conflict would wax and wane. It would wax when I would meet or listen to senior members of the classics or history departments. It would wane when I was immersed in researching and writing about mental retardation, anxiety, and the clinical situation. And even when it waned, Schaefer was in my head reminding me of my ignorance of people, eras, problems, and traditions that as a student of human behavior I should and needed to know. I knew that our world was not born yesterday, but that is about all I knew. I read voluminously and indiscriminately, but it was untutored reading. Schaefer was out in California, and I was a beginning assistant professor at Yale. The only solace I had derived from the fact, which I successfully kept secret, was that I knew I was by classical standards the uneducated American. I judged myself, then as today, not by a relative but by an absolute standard.

A second benefit I derived from Schaefer was a heightened sensitivity to the obvious: You are what you are because, among other things, you are an American and not a German, or Englishman, or Frenchman. If you want to understand yourself or others, you cannot ignore the fact that you have been socialized into a particular society or one of its distinctive parts. The differences are reflected in language, behavior, and worldview, differences that have to be understood before they are judged, although these differences predispose us to judge and to bypass understanding. To someone like Schaefer, these differences were not abstractions but stimuli to understanding. Interested (indeed, obsessed) as he was in art in myriad societies and cultures—how and why they differed in content, style, and level of artistic achievement—his task was to understand these differences in the terms of each distinctive society and culture. Schaefer was more than an art historian, a type about whom he had very mixed feelings. He was a historian of cultures. Schaefer was the first person to force me to confront the implications of the fact that I was American. He never did this directly, but it was impossible to be with him and not be aware that we were dramatically different kinds of people in part because he was German and I was American. It was the differences that fascinated me. One incident stands out, an incident that on the surface may seem trivial and comic but to me made the cultural differences between German him and American me real.

It was in 1943, several months after Schaefer had married an American woman, his second wife. We had a date to go to the Metropolitan Museum in New York. I was to come to his apartment, meet his new wife, and then go to the museum. I had two immediate reactions when I entered the apartment. The first was that Gudrun was as gracious and sensitive a woman as I had ever met. In personality and appearance, she resembled Eleanor Roosevelt. The second reaction was that the electricity of conflict suffused the air. Obviously, there had been a quarrel. After about 10 minutes, Schaefer realized my discomfort (and his own), and he said, "Seymour, I want you to listen to what happened yesterday and to give your honest opinion." On the previous day, one of Gudrun's best friends from another state had come to visit and to meet Schaefer. According to Schaefer, she breezed into the apartment and when introduced to him exclaimed, "Henry, it is a pleasure to meet you."

Finished with his account, he looked at me and asked, "What do you think of *that*?" I looked at him blankly, expecting him to continue the story, to clarify the question. He saw my puzzlement, a puzzled look appeared on his face, and finally he blurted, "She called me *Henry. You* don't even call me Henry." Having taken a year of German, I vaguely knew that the use of *du* and *sie* depended on the depth of a relationship, and, therefore, for a complete stranger to call Schaefer Henry was unforgivably gross. I contained my inner laughter only because I realized, fortunately, that I was witness to a misunderstanding produced by two different ways of viewing social relationships, only one of the ways such views shaped relationships. The incident, of course, said a lot about Schaefer's personality, but to stop there would be to trivialize the implications of it. As a clinician, I had been taught that my task was to understand a patient in his or her terms. Nothing in my education and training had exposed me to applying the principle to individuals culturally different from me. Psychology was psychology, anthropology was anthropology, and putting them together was not an obligation of psychology! If my undergraduate education was far from classical, my professional education and training were even more parochial in terms of understanding diversity of human behavior in diverse cultures.

And that brings me to the Hampton Cafeteria on Madison Avenue in Manhattan. The cafeteria no longer exists, but when it did, it was the eating-meeting place of as heterogeneous a collection of Europeans as one could imagine, all part of the New York art dealers' scene. Germans, Austrians, Italians, French—each talking in his or her language and each frequently replying in his or her native tongue without a break in the conversation. Because I was with Schaefer, they assumed that I understood what they were talking about. When they found out otherwise, and given my youth, they would frequently stop to explain to me why the conversation was as heated as it was. They were art dealers, but the range of their interests was to me phenomenal. If I had any tendency, which I did not, to overevaluate my education, the seminars in the Hampton cafeteria extinguished it. It was there that I began to learn that when an American is called a cosmopolitan, it does not mean the same as in Europe, where the worldview of the intellectual cosmopolitan encompasses many nations, and the intellectual arena transcends national boundaries. At the same time that I was proud of the fact that America had given these Europeans a refuge, and I was convinced that we would be their beneficiaries, I was bothered by the thought that the traditions that had shaped them found inhospitable soil in this country. Their worldview not only transcended national boundaries but was rooted in a present that had continuities spanning centuries and millennia. If in subsequent years I came to revere William James and John Dewey, it was because they were, *in my field*, the best examples of the intellectual cosmopolitan in the European tradition. No two people could be more American, but that was no bar to forging the broadest of worldviews.

The world of art: that is the world Schaefer opened for me. He took me to museums, stood me before paintings and sculpture, forced me to study what I saw and to articulate my judgments, which then became the focus of discussion. On one such occasion, he stood me before a painting of a rural scene by Poussin. This was early in our trips, and my ignorance and biases were all too clear. I responded unreflectively by saying, "I don't like farm scenes." Schaefer looked down on me and said in a stern but fatherly way, "Your first job when you look at a work of art is to try to identify *the artistic problem* the artist was trying to overcome. The artistic process is a struggle involving color, form, composition, size, and content. Each painting has its own problems, some more difficult than others. We owe it to the artist, regardless of his level of development of visual conceiving, to judge his work in terms of what he wanted to accomplish." He then went on to say, "Study that painting with this question in mind: Can you change this or that color, this or that line, without changing anything else?" I studied the painting for some time, and it was as if a new world was opening before my eyes. If I changed this or that, I would have to change a lot else. I knew what a gestalt is in a way that I had never comprehended before! Schaefer went on to explain that when we look at a painting on a museum wall, we are looking at a final product that was preceded by a series of sketches, which could be voluminous, the purpose of which was to identify and attempt to resolve the inevitable problems and discrepancies that arise between internal vision or conception and the realities of color, line, size, and composition. This was (he would say in his own way) no stimulus and response, no cause and effect, but a constant back and forth, a totality of experience that included the artist and his materials, both of which were always changing. For some time, I became engrossed in viewing the sketches that led up to a painting before me, endlessly fascinated, then as now, by the cognitive struggle, the problem-solving aspects, the emergence of order, the creation of a configurated vision, that the artistic process required. I had seen this take place in Schaefer's studio at Southbury: the struggles of the residents, throwing away or tearing up one paper and starting over with a new one, the look of satisfaction when they liked what they had done, the frustration when they did not like or saw a mess in what they had done—all part of a total immersion, in Dewey's sense of the concept of *an experience.* Although Schaefer would tell me that what I was observing was in principle exactly the same as that experienced by more highly developed artists, that the artistic process has its own requirements wherever that process is found, I never grasped the generality of what he said until we started to go to museums.

Schaefer forever changed the way I look at, study, and judge a work of art, regardless of the level of development of the artist. But that is stating my debt in too narrow terms, because in truth Schaefer provided me with a view of human potential that I had long sought but never found. It was more than a view or belief or act of faith. I had observed that potential where it was not supposed to exist. He had demonstrated to my eyes enough "data" for me to accept as highly probable that creative artistic activity was a universal human capacity. And what I learned from him was grist for my own experiential mill: the nature of our social world either does not recognize or it extinguishes that and other capacities. Schaefer knew that, of course, just as he knew that what his students accomplished was not independent of him and the contexts he created for them. But that knowledge was to him of secondary importance to the demonstration in case after case, in the present and the historical past, of the unfolding of the stages of visual conceiving in the creation of works of art. What was of secondary importance to him was primary to me, but without his influence, the basis for my convictions, the scope of my outlook, would be incomparably more parochial than it is.

I have spent countless days in classrooms in and after Southbury. From the time of my relationship with Schaefer, there was hardly an instance when I would not find myself comparing the behavior of students in those classrooms with that of those in Schaefer's studio. In the one setting, I saw a pouring in of information, student passivity, rote memorizing, and an emphasis on outcome (the *right* answer) and token gestures to process. In the other, I saw struggle, eagerness, and perseverance in the effort to put "out there" a visual conception in tune with and satisfying to the eye of the creator: changing, distorting, simplifying external reality in a configurated way. In the one, individuality was hard to discern; in the other, it hit you in the face.

What Schaefer's studio represented to the residents, Southbury represented to me. No one was telling me what to do and how to do it. Although I was on my own in the middle of rural nowhere, I had Schaefer and my wife, Esther, to stimulate and support me. I had the sense of growth and development, the sense that I was giving expression to my abilities and interests, sensitive to the "real world" around me but nevertheless intent on understanding and changing that world. I was not about to be judged by conventional external standards of what psychology and psychologists were supposed to be. Unlike the residents whom Schaefer chose as students, I was semi-spoiled. Indirectly but powerfully, all that Schaefer stood for and did served as warning of the dangers of being spoiled and as stimulus to going my own way. He was the greatest of my teachers.

The day before this chapter was finished, I was visited by two people, Bruce and Cathy Thomas, whom I had never met personally but with whom I had carried on a professional correspondence for several years. In the course of the conversation, they asked me about the role of Schaefer in my professional development. I had forgotten that in a letter I had suggested that they look at Schaefer's book in light of their interest in education and its inadequacies. When I asked whether they had seen the book, their faces lit up, and they tried to convey to me the impact the book had had on them. (The last time someone had taken the book out of the library had been 10 years earlier, and apparently only one other person had read it from the time it was purchased.) Their reaction was identical to that of others to whom I had recommended the book. You really have to see before you begin to consider believing. Language is dull brass for describing works of art.

I reprint below a letter I received from Kevin Whitnaw, a student of Schaefer's. Mr. Whitnaw visited me in New Haven, and he projected onto a screen slides showing the development of several of his students. The development of the students was nothing less than staggering. Mr. Whitnaw obviously is a great teacher, but alone, like Schaefer was.

> Dear Dr. Sarason:
>
> I am delighted that you are going to do a chapter on Henry's work at Southbury. This would be most valuable for several reasons, chief of which is to give an intimate and well-documented look at Henry's actual pedagogical method and how that method found integration in the psychological sphere of mental retardation. Also valuable for the many who value *The Unfolding of Artistic Activity* would be your commentary as to the mise-en-scene, so to speak, which produced the book—the complex interactions of yourself, Henry, and the participating patients there. It would be interesting for people to know in more detail what psychological changes manifested (and how they manifested) in someone like Selma. Henry told me something about it years ago, but I have forgotten the details.
>
> As I mentioned in my first letter, *The Unfolding* has been out for 36 years and it has not changed art education. Henry himself, in his lifetime, became deeply discouraged over the failure of the art education academy in this country to take serious note of his book. He told me in 1971: "I have often the temptation to throw up the whole thing (his art education work and the publishing of his great book on *The Essence of the Art Form*). I could go to Europe by the next plane. There I could look at exhibitions and enjoy art and live a completely different kind of life. But I have, I might say, a kind of

guilty conscience in the face of such thought. I have a responsibility in full conscience to do this work." And I said: "And if you had not published *The Unfolding of Artistic Activity*"—he broke in: "Yes, but not more than ten people in the whole world understood that book"—And I interrupted: ". . . then my life would have been inexpressibly poorer, and I would have been diminished if you had kept the book a secret and written it, yet simply put it away." These are exact quotes from a conversation I had with him on the subject of exhibiting art. He had become so discouraged with the general art scene at this point that he did not even wish to have his own students exhibit work!

You see, Dr. Sarason, Henry suffered a great deal of ignominy, spite, misunderstanding, neglect and downright hostility from established academic art educators. He was extremely sensitive to this, especially so, since he himself was a professional in education, fully qualified, and a great teacher whose students produced work of outstanding quality. He was good, and he knew it. He had something of utmost importance to offer to educators, psychologists, artists, architects and laymen, to mention only a few categories.

But, with the advent of Abstract Expressionism in the 1950's and the steady rise of a kind of graphic and pictorial work which was profoundly anti-Gestalt, the temper of the times was against his implementation of the hard-won conclusions which make up his book, his work and his life. He had told me: "When I left Europe I looked at the continent receding over the horizon and I took a solemn oath that I would take this Idea to the United States and make it a living Reality." He fulfilled this oath by publishing *The Unfolding* and by the productive years which followed in the forties and the fifties. But, as he got better, the general art scene got worse! He would go to Europe in the summer and there be told by young art students that the old Gothic painters like Grunewald and Durer (if there *are* any like them!) were nothing but "old nonsense."

When Henry died I asked the responsible parties at St. Mary's College to put on an event which would review and sum up his achievement as a writer, thinker, and active art educator. Somehow, this never got done, I don't know why, and it always bothered me that such a man should thus slip, unnoticed and unacclaimed, out of this world. Perhaps one of the reasons for the hostility and neglect which he suffered was the fact that excellence in a field is not always admired, but often envied. Also the fact that he was never noted for his tact and had little of the small talk and social personality so useful in the educational field. He was passionately devoted to The Artistic Form and he was delighted when he found another who shared that passion. And he had little time for anything else.

The temper of the times has changed. People are beginning to understand that anti-gestalt pictorial products have nothing to do with art in its most fundamental, ancient and highest sense. Many professionals are beginning to see that *quality* is the hallmark of artistic excellence and indeed excellence in any field, whether it be psychology, artisanship or architecture. Recently, my wife and I had the good luck to meet a fine architect, world-renowned, currently engaged in building a university in Japan. He is also a professor at the University of California, but not too busy to take an interest in the project of building a house and studios for us here in Northern California. He lives in Berkeley, and when I met him I mentioned that Schaefer-Simmern used to live a few blocks away, and that his books had reminded me of the ideas in *The Unfolding*. Well, Dr. Sarason, this man caught on fire! He said when he was studying architecture at Harvard that he had read *The Unfolding* every day and had kept it by him as a source book. But he had no idea that Schaefer-Simmern had lived in Berkeley, or that his work had continued at all after the publication of the book. He has very kindly offered to sponsor a lecture for me at the University of California.

Now, then, the reason I suggested the lecture to you: I did so because I was reasonably certain that there are also many people at Yale, faculty and students in art, in education, in psychology and philosophy who would be deeply interested in the visual results of Henry's long career as well as the pedagogical means by which these came into being. When I lecture and show the slides, people are amazed. They can't believe that work of such outstanding quality, and such a radically simple approach to art can be such a well kept secret. They are also astonished to learn of the existence of *The Unfolding* and that it is still in print.

There is also the paradoxical factor of diminishing returns as time races onward. When Henry told me in 1971 that only ten people in the world understood this book, he was speaking correctly. Now, 12 years later, I am sorry to reckon that those numbers have shrunk. As far as I know there are no young people who have taken up this Idea with the vigor and conviction which will make it operable to future generations. There is, thus, a certain urgency, depending on our viewpoint. Quite possibly, the availability of *The Unfolding* may be lost for many generations and only rediscovered years hence by some group or individual. In this case they would have to reconstruct it from the external evidence inward—no easy task! But I think such a creative hiatus would be a pity since it is the living instruction that gets the message across, and there are still a few left who worked directly with Henry, having grasped the pedagogical method in their bones, so to speak, and thus can transmit it without distortion.

But my reason for writing you was simpler still: You were with Henry in the old days and you helped him get his book written, both by your active cooperation and your true understanding of what he was doing. Above all, he needed that understanding and in you he had it. You are one of the ten people who understand the book. He told me that. So, you see, when I heard that you were doing some writing about Henry I thought the least I could do would be to offer you a lecture. And though the materials I show are not specifically about mental retardation, they apply (as you well know) with equal force on the scale of measurable "intelligence" up or down. Selma was no genius, but look what she produced! I show slides of her work to my eight-year-olds and tell them about Selma and the discipline she brought to her art. My children can relate directly to her work and feel strong encouragement through her example.

Anyway, I wanted *you* to see the kind of achievements which have flowered since *The Unfolding of Artistic Activity* was published, both for specific application in your field of expertise and for the larger frame of reference where psychology relates directly to the human potential.

Again, thanks for your letter.

Sincere regards,
Kevin Whitnaw

Here are the significances I draw from the Schaefer story:

- He knew his subject matter (backward and forward) which included how the learner thinks about, approaches, and engages in the activity, and he also knew that these factors very likely reflect the "messages" the person has absorbed from diverse external sources about the nature and purpose of the activity and how its products will be judged. There was no dividing line between the person and what is conventionally called the curriculum or subject matter.
- He knew his subject matter well enough to know when, where, or why the individual may encounter difficulties. He did not provide answers

to these difficulties, and he never showed a person the "correct" answer. He trusted and encouraged the person to think about, study, and judge what he or she had done. For Schaefer, the person was able to do and critique the end product; he never confused memory with thinking. It was Schaefer's obligation to respect, stimulate, and support a person's capacity for judgment as a basis for change; he was a prodder, a stimulator, not a shower.

- By words and personal style—his gentleness, the seriousness and interest with which he took the person and their artistic product—he engendered trust of and respect for him. They felt safe with him, safe enough to articulate thought and feeling about what they were experiencing. He was believable, he was not acting, he was there for them.
- But Schaefer knew he was in a performing role which required him to establish a relationship which would allow the other person to feel Schaefer truly understood him or her. He identified with the other person at the same time that he was never in doubt that he was performing. I never asked him how he could be gentle, psychologically sensitive to, and endlessly patient with the Southbury residents and be otherwise in most of his other relationships. There was always a part of Schaefer who knew precisely what he was doing and why. He may have appeared totally immersed in his role but he was not. Like a good performing artist there was a part of him observing himself in a role which required performing in certain ways.

Initially, I had serious reservations about Schaefer's conceptions and goals. What led me to begin to think otherwise was that I could relate them to personal experience from my past. What had seemed to be theory and abstraction took on concrete meaning which made me want to learn more from Schaefer. Here, too, I had reservations. Just as I could not imagine him interacting productively with long-institutionalized mentally retarded individuals, I doubted whether the two of us could hit it off because he was so serious, so single minded, so fitting my stereotype of a rigid, unbending Prussian. And he was to me an intellectually intimidating individual. Why did he take to me? Why did he come to be over the years so eager and willing to be my friend as well as my mentor about art and art history? In the course of rereading the chapter I wrote about him, I think I have much of the answer. The Southbury residents did not have the words to convey that they were unspoiled and ignoramuses in matters of artistic activity. By words, manner, and style I conveyed just that to Schaefer. I wanted to know him, understand him, and learn from him because I sensed that what I would learn had significance for problems and questions in other spheres of my interests. What I would learn about art and art history would have relevance for me beyond art and history; it would not be confined to those categories, it would be of practical importance, not an isolated subject matter which, however interesting, is bounded and confined, unrelated to anything else in my intellectual and personal life. Schaefer viewed me no differently than his willing Southbury residents, and he came to feel as close to me as he was to them, as devoted to them as he was to me, as gentle, giving, and serious with them as he was with me. He started where I was, which was near ground zero, and he patiently moved me forward. When years after he died I dedicated my book *The Challenge of Art to Psychology* (1990a) to him, I was repaying a personal and intellectual debt. Not the least aspect of that debt was that he helped me understand the difference between contexts of productive and unproductive learning; In the former the teacher is a creative performer who captures her audience, in the latter the teacher leaves the audience psychologically unmoved and motivationally impoverished, dutifully playing the memory game which, when play is over, is soon forgotten because it is so unrelated to the rest of the student's lived experience.

Should we encourage students, say in fourth or fifth grade, to be creative poets? Should we encourage old, sick, disabled, lonely, dispirited residents of a nursing home to be creative poets? That is what poet Kenneth Koch did, first in a Spanish Harlem school, and then in a nursing home in New York's lower east side. He describes these efforts in two books (Koch, 1970, 1977) which the reader will find inspiring and instructive because the similarities between Schaefer and Koch's ways of thinking, relating, and performing are striking.

The obligations of the teacher are several. First, to know the subject matter well enough to be able to pinpoint when or where the student may have difficulty. Second, to engender and sustain a relationship in which the student feels respected and understood and safe enough to be able to give voice to thoughts and feelings about self *and* the subject matter, and in giving voice in words, facial expression, or body language adds to the teacher's understanding of that child's attitudes toward and understanding of the significance of subject matter. Third, and implied in the first two, the teacher not only has to make the creative effort to identify with how the student of that age or grade is likely to think but also to make his or her understanding believable and reassuring. The fourth is that the teacher must never lose sight of the consequences of the positive and negative self-fulfilling prophecies. What undergirds the positive self-fulfilling stance are two assumptions: the bedrock belief (1) that the individual is capable of learning this or that operation or subject matter and (2) that the teacher has a conception, a way, an approach that will develop and exploit that capability, assumptions that Schaefer and Koch obviously accepted. Undergirding the negative self-fulfilling stance is the belief that the person is not capable of learning this or that, and on the basis of that belief the teacher responds in ways that ensure the person will be incapable. The readers of this book who are familiar with the history of societal expectations of women will grasp the differences between the two types of self-fulfilling prophecies. They are differences that make a difference. This, I should hasten to add, does not mean that either stance is so intrinsically valid or so powerful in their consequences as to say that this or that level of outcome will occur. In the realm of human affairs that is truly asking far too much.

Let us now turn to what I think all this means for the selection and preparation of teachers. Again I expect that there will be those who will view what I will suggest as impractical, untested, and requiring a time perspective we cannot afford to adopt. If by untested is meant that I can present no evidence based on credible research for what I will suggest, I have to agree, even though my critics cannot present evidence that how teachers are selected and prepared today has its intended outcomes. Whatever changes in selection and preparation that have been instituted in the last 50 years have not only been cosmetic, but regressive as well. But it is pointless and fruitless to engage in the "you accuse me of x at the same time you are guilty of x" type of argument. If you believe the present way teachers are selected and prepared is very unsatisfactory (and if you have not, you should read, as I suggested earlier, the 1996 report of the National Commission on Teaching and America's Future, prepared with Linda Darling-Hammond as Executive Director), you may find what I have to say interesting (in a positive way). If you believe that all is well or not worrisomely bad, it may be that you should read no further.

CHAPTER 8

The Selection of Teachers

In the health section of the *New York Times* for December 23, 1997, there is a long article by Susan Gilbert, the headline for which is "Forget About Bedside Manners, Some Doctors Have No Manners." The article discusses recent surveys indicating that a majority of physicians handle their transactions with patients and their families, especially when the diagnosis is serious and inevitably upsetting, in an insensitive, problem-producing way. In my book *Caring and Compassion in Clinical Practice* (Sarason, 1985), I give many examples in line with these recent surveys, but I restrict myself here to a personal one:

> I came to visit my mother in her hospital room a week after she had been operated on for lymphatic cancer, a major site of which was behind the thyroid gland. Speech was impossible for her, because of both the surgery and an emergency tracheotomy 2 days later. We had been told that there might be temporary interference with speech. When I entered her room, she was crying and visibly agitated. I called the nurse, who could offer no explanation. Finally, my mother indicated that she wanted pencil and paper. The message she wrote said that, just before I had arrived, the surgeon had appeared, accompanied by several interns and residents. He explained to his younger colleagues my mother's condition, the type of surgery that had been performed, and that it had been necessary to sever several major vocal chords—following which he and the others left the room. That was how my mother found out that she would never talk above a whisper.

That, I shall assume, is an extreme case, but it is not a rare one. Indeed, Gilbert's article emphasizes that a substantial number of physicians admit that their training for how to be with and talk to patients and families is trivial in time and worthless in its consequences.

I start with these recent surveys for several reasons. The first is that I spent a good part of the first two decades of my professional career (1942–62) trying to cope with parents still suffering from the substance and manner with which the diagnosis of their child's mental retardation had been given them. The fact is that in my first book *Psychological Problems in Mental Deficiency* (Sarason, 1948) there is a chapter critical of the training of physicians in regard to their insensitivity in communicating to parents a most fateful diagnosis. Needless to say, what I wrote and what others wrote in subsequent decades had no impact whatsoever on medical education. If anything, matters are worse today because the economic structure of medicine, plus the ever-increasing pressure to acquire technical skills and to assimilate hordes of facts, are used to justify giving little or no time to matters psychological. That is an excuse, not an explanation. It sidesteps an important problem by ignoring it. It makes a virtue of a perceived necessity by bulwarking a status quo whose audience increasingly sees the "performers" in negative terms.

What I say about medical education applies to the preparation of teachers. In the post World War II era the most significant change in preparatory programs of teachers has been an increase in subject matter requirements (more courses), a decrease in emphasis on pedagogical theory and method (the so-called "Mickey Mouse" courses), at the same time continuing to ignore the nature of the obligation of the teacher to take seriously who the learner is, where the learner is coming from, and how to use such knowledge to make subject matter interesting, motivating, and compelling—as Mr. Holland learned to do the hard way. We are used to hearing that physicians should treat people, not diagnostic categories; they should be as concerned with preventing problems as with repairing them. In education we are told that teachers should teach students, not subject matter, which is to say that not taking individuality seriously is a surefire way of subverting the productive assimilation of subject matter. Riveting on subject matter is like an actor reading a script to the audience. Whether teacher or actor, the performer has to "move" the audience. Between performer and audience is far more than a formal, predetermined script, just as between physician and patient there is more than a litany of symptoms.

There is a maxim among personnel specialists that if you know how to select, you have licked 50% of the training problem. But that maxim only makes practical sense when three conditions exist. The first, of course, is that you have an empirically validated understanding of what the position requires for successful performance; you employ (or should employ) criteria demonstrably correlated with performance. You do not employ criteria that do no better than tossing a coin, or worse. And again, of course, you are or should be ever alert to the possibility that your criteria do not omit a performance characteristic the position requires. For example, if the criteria for admission to medical schools contain *nothing* relevant to the capacity for caring, compassionate behavior, even though the absence of that behavior is a source of public criticism and complaint, should not that omission be rectified to the extent it is possible? Criteria for selection are the consequence of a developmental process the goal of which is to improve the practical value of selection; it is or should be a self-correcting process. That developmental process takes time, work, and acceptance of the moral and scientific obligation to do justice both to the requirements of the position and those seeking to attain it. Selection is not about gambling, it is about the lives of people. If inevitably—and I use that word advisedly—selection criteria fall short of the mark of perfection, often far short, it does not absolve us from trying to do better than we do, especially if utilizing the criteria enables us to do only somewhat better than tossing a coin.

The second condition in which the maxim makes practical sense is when you have far more applicants than there are positions and, therefore, you must be very clear what your selection criteria should be. Where the candidate pool is large and the number of presumed excellent candidates larger than the number of positions, the clarity, relevance, and validity of the criteria become crucial. For example, years back the dean of the Yale Law School told me that if they chose for admission only from among those who were Phi Beta Kappas, they had ten times more candidates than they had openings. How *do* you choose I asked? His answer essentially was that choosing was the responsibility of an admission committee and thank God he was not on that committee! He was quick to add that the committee's choices were far from perfect but that to seek to determine how the selection process could be improved would require too much time and money not justified by the degree of improvement that might be expected. That judgment was not shared by another equally renowned member of the law faculty who said, "The Yale Law School, *like all similar law schools*, is a trade school which attracts very bright students, many of whom are not thinkers, let alone creative ones, but who know what a Yale Law School degree means in the marketplace. They will be competent lawyers, although there will be some who will not be, but competence is far less than the Yale Law School says it wants its graduates to be." Another member of the faculty said that the law school could be very selective in light of the large pool of applicants "but no one is dissatisfied enough to push for changes in our selection criteria." If a large pool of applicants gives one the luxury to be selective, it does not necessarily mean that the criteria employed are as valid as they could be. (Later in this chapter I shall discuss the situation where the applicant pool is not large.)

The third condition in which the maxim is crucially and obviously distinctive is one in which conventional criteria like grades or test scores or degree of motivation play a minor role, which is not to say they play no role at all. Prototypical are programs in the performing arts. In the *New York Times* for March 21, 1998, on the first page, there is an article by Ralph Blumenthal with the headline "So You Want to Be a Star? Then Get in Line." The stimulus for the article was the increasing size of the pool of applicants for admission to university programs. "Juilliard, perhaps the most selective performing arts school in the nation, is sorting through 1,100 acting applications for its 20 positions, up 10% from last year." At New York University's Tisch School, the largest *undergraduate* drama department in the world, 2,200 applicants were competing for 350 freshman openings in 1998, up from 1,518 in 1997, 1,262 in 1996, and 880 in 1993. At the University of Delaware's graduate theater program the 500 applications for a class of 38 represented a 20% jump. The rise in other universities is more modest. The Yale School of Drama accepts 17 applicants from a pool of around 800.

We can assume that for each applicant to a graduate or undergraduate program the school requires test scores, grades, letters of recommendation, and relevant performing experience. For graduate programs, previous performing experience is essential. We also can assume, especially for graduate programs, and as the article indicates, that *no student is selected without an audition.*[1] *To members of these programs it is a glimpse of the obvious that before you select a candidate you had better see how they perform.* This is not to say that they expect a polished performance. Far from it, they know they are observing untrained individuals, but they regard it as irresponsible both to student and program not to have a direct basis for judging whether the individual has the qualities performing requires. Granted those judgments are subjective, but they are judgments based on considerable experience. They would not deny the subjectivity (how could they?), but they would vigorously deny that selecting only on the basis of conventional "objective" data is justifiable on moral or educational grounds. Their basic axiom can be put this way: If you want to predict who will make a good actor, you have to see them act, keeping in mind you are observing an amateur.

Auditions are not interviews. They are samples of behavior in a role the individual has been asked to assume or in one of his or her own choosing; either way, the individual seeks to demonstrate that he or she understands the role and can manifest that understanding on the level of action.

---

1. These programs obviously cannot audition all applicants. We do not know how they reduce the pool to manageable proportions. As best as I can determine, they reduce the pool to two or three times the number of openings.

The task of the auditor (or auditors) is to discern those features of voice, bearing, expressiveness, and understanding which suggest a potential for creative growth as an actor. If you ask auditors, as I have sometimes done, how secure they are in their judgments and how well auditors agree with each other, the answers, put together and paraphrased, go like this: "If you are asking if we make mistakes, we first have to agree about what we mean by *mistakes*. If you mean we rejected someone who went elsewhere and became a competent or more than competent actor, then we have to say we make mistakes, and perhaps not a few. If you mean by *a mistake* that among those we select there are complete duds, then we make very, very few mistakes. Bear in mind that *all* of our applicants have had acting experience in school, or college, in a community theater, or in a summer camp for the performing arts. They regard themselves as actors. By and large they are self-confident youngsters convinced they have what it takes to be an actor, to be in the theater. So, when we invite them to come for an audition, we are their audience and we adopt a 'show me' stance. Better yet, a 'surprise me' stance: Am I struck by something I did not expect, something unusual and positive, seeds we can help develop? Do auditors disagree among themselves? Rarely, but when there is a disagreement, it does not bode well for the applicant."

What an applicant says about him- or herself and what others say about that person in letters of recommendation are not to be ignored, but the rationale for the audition rests on an assumption that everyday life forces us to accept as a fact: what a person says he or she can do is far from correlated with what that person does do. Sometimes we are pleasantly surprised by the discrepancy, other times we are dismayed. When we form a positive impression about someone on the basis of talking with them (for example, in an interview), we tend to assume that our favorable impression would be confirmed if we saw what that person does in other arenas. And we tend to do the same when our impression is a negative one. Let me give an illustration of the latter from personal experience. It was, like the experience involving Schaefer-Simmern in Chapter 7, most instructive for me.

It was back in the early 1960s. I had been asked by New Haven's school superintendent to spend 2 or 3 days a week *in the classrooms* of a 100-year-old ghetto school to help teachers with students who were management problems. I initially met with the teachers as a group and then individually, explaining my role and emphasizing that how they used me, if at all, was up to them. All of the teachers were quite aware that the educational and behavioral performance of the students had brought the school much criticism. Both in the groups and in individual meetings the teachers spoke nostalgically about the good old days when the students came from very different ethnic backgrounds (Italian and Jewish). The most complaining, vociferous teacher was a woman in her sixties who looked (and I learned later was) frail and sickly. I had difficulty inhibiting my reaction to her not-so-subtle insensitive, racist remarks. After the initial group meeting I told the teachers I would let them know when I would visit their classroom. I had already decided that I would see Mrs. Treadow only after I had visited all the other classrooms. I had visions of how her classroom would be, and I was not at all sure I could deal with her racism. The long and short of it is that after several visits I had to conclude that she was one of the most creative, demanding, *and supportive* teachers I had ever seen. For example, she would throw out a question to the class, the children would raise and vigorously wave their hands to be called on, and Mrs. Treadow would then pick out a student to give an answer. Not infrequently the answer was wrong, at which point the other children would again energetically wave their hands. Mrs. Treadow would tell them to lower their hands and in a quiet, patient, non-demeaning way would stay with that student until both of them determined where he or she had gone astray. I never have seen a teacher do that. Socratic describes her. Mrs. Treadow also had a closet full of games and puzzles which she had devised and built as tools which were not only interesting to children but were aids in learning to read and sharpen arithmetic skills. The school had no gym, but she said, "No one should expect third graders to sit all day without physical activity." So sickly and frail Mrs. Treadow spent 10 minutes twice a day doing exercise games *with* the students. It was funny and poignant to see her join in the exercises. No other teacher in the school did that. Finally, she did not consider any of her students behavioral or serious educational problems. After several visits I had to agree. Indeed, I was relieved, I had more than enough to keep me busy in the other classrooms. I should point out that I subsequently learned that unlike any of the other teachers the achievement test scores of her students were above national norms and that had been true in previous years.

   Listening to Mrs. Treadow was one thing, seeing her in action was quite another. The teachers in that school had not invited me there. As one would expect, they resented being singled out by the superintendent, although they never said that out loud. From their standpoint they were being auditioned and judged, even though I had assured them otherwise. I would under no circumstances report my conclusions, let alone any recommendations, to the superintendent or any other administrator. Nevertheless, the teachers saw themselves as auditioners and me as the auditor. And the truth is that I was an auditor. What about the other teachers? Were my initial impressions of them predictive of what I would observe in the classrooms? The fact is that with one exception I regarded them as friendly, likeable, and dedicated; as teachers they did not hold a candle to Mrs. Treadow. The exception was a woman who struck me immediately as immature, lost, and without any semblance of self-confidence. A woman in her forties, she was a frightened child. Her classroom was chaos. It was in her classroom that I saw a boy climb the walls via exposed floor-to-ceiling steam pipes. The most positive thing I did for the students in that school was over a period of months convince her that she should ask to be transferred to another school. Her transfer was greeted with relief by everyone. She should never have become a teacher, and she should never have been allowed to remain one. (Although I was tempted to go to the superintendent, I knew that that would be going back on the agreement I had made and would complicate, if not end, my relationship with the other teachers.)

How are teachers selected for preparatory programs? What criteria do they employ? Whether the program is graduate or undergraduate, attention is given to course grades, a test of intellectual ability, an interview, letters of recommendation. There is no audition and for two reasons. The first is that candidates have had no prior teaching experience, although I assume there are the usual "here and there" exceptions. But that point raises this question: Granted they are without teaching experience, are there not characteristics of a "good" teacher which can be observed in an appropriately designed format in which the candidate interacts with children? Such formats, of course, have to be developed and tested. There is no a priori basis whatsoever for assuming that such formats are unnecessary or unhelpful, a waste of time and energy. Such an assumption makes sense only if there is evidence that current selection procedures are doing what they are supposed to do: To select individuals deemed capable of understanding, motivating, guiding the intellectual and social-personal development of children, and to "select out" those whose personality and style will turn students off rather than on, who will stifle children's curiosity rather than capitalizing on it, who command rather than lead, who are too constricted and concerned with power and authority to be sensitive to individual differences among students. I have never heard a knowledgeable person in the educational community assert that preparatory programs have a good track record in selecting candidates, and that is putting it mildly.[2]

---

2. In *any* selection procedure for *any* position which is *demonstrably* valid it is illegitimate to conclude that those who are not selected possess no characteristics, personal or otherwise, which would be virtues in another type of role. But when, as in the case of the selection of candidates for teaching, there is a clear indication that those selected contain an uncomfortable number of what are called "false positives," it is justified proposing ways of improving selection. I shall shortly indicate why the problem of "false negatives" in teacher selection is far less of a practical issue.

The second reason auditions are not considered—more correctly, not even thought of—is that the applicant pool for preparatory programs is not large and it is no secret that these programs are under pressure to take in sufficient numbers to justify the program's costs and existence. That kind of pressure results in admitting individuals of borderline quality, using the usual criteria. That pressure, in part, also explains why the rejection rate in these programs hovers around 17%, a figure dramatically below that for the conventional performing arts. I am not aware of any comparative data for the conventional performing arts and teaching indicating the number of students who are asked to leave the programs because, for one or another reason, they are deemed unfit for the role. I have had direct experience with several teacher preparatory programs, and I have talked with faculty in many other programs. I had to conclude that termination from the program was truly insignificant in number even though program supervisors had serious doubts about more than a few students. This is not because of financial pressure alone but also because the faculty is reluctant to make a decision they know will impact negatively upon a student's career plans and sense of personal worthiness. That reluctance is understandable but unlike the case with other performing arts, these borderline (or less) students will embark on a career in which what they do or do not do will affect two or more generations of children.

For 17 years I served on the graduate admission committee for Yale's department of psychology. From an applicant pool of 500–600, we would select 20–30 students. There was no financial pressure to admit *at least* this or that number. From each applicant we had grades, GRE scores, letters of recommendation, and a personal statement about why he or she thought they were suited for a career in psychology. Using those data we could have selected two or three times the number we admitted (if we had a correspondingly larger faculty). In the spring of each year the department reviewed all students. There was never a year when there was not a long, agonizing discussion about at least seven or eight students for whom there were serious reservations about their continuation. Occasionally the number was higher. Those meetings would last several hours because one or two members of the faculty moved to terminate these questionable students. We rarely terminated a student. "Let's try to figure out how we can help them. Let's give them another year. Maybe they will come around." Far more often than not they did not "come around." And we would repeat the agony the next year, which is why as the years went on we had a group I called "student emeritus." I found it both ironic and amusing that a department deservedly acknowledged to be research-oriented would never alter or seriously question its selection procedures. We should not be too hard on teacher preparatory programs with small applicant pools and financial pressures to select *x* number of students. Four fifths of the students in our department were in specialty areas not involving sustained contact with and influence upon children in schools; if these areas contained questionable students, at least one did not have to be concerned, or not very concerned, that in their futures they would cause harm to school children. But in the case of teacher preparatory programs, that has to be the overriding concern.

There was an interval in the early post World War II years when, because of the baby boom, preparatory programs for teachers had a large pool of applicants. Schools were being built at a rate redolent of airplane construction during the war. At least one school in Connecticut went on double session the day it opened. If it is an exaggeration to say that criteria for selection of teachers went by the boards, it is not much of an exaggeration. During that same interval there began a cascade of criticism—in what has been called "The Great Debate"—of schools of education in general and preparatory programs for teachers in particular. The major criticisms of these programs were that (1) students were not sufficiently steeped in the subject matter they would teach and (2) on average those who were selected were intellectually undistinguished, if not inferior. That is to say, the more you know and the brighter you are, the better you will be as a teacher.[3] For those criticisms its proponents did not (and could not) present credible evidence. But what the critics said led a fair number of elite private colleges and universities to offer Master of Arts in Teaching programs in which post-baccalaureate students would obtain a far more extensive and firm grasp of subject matter than in the usual undergraduate program, and it was claimed that these students would be selected by criteria ensuring higher intellectual ability. As the turbulent sixties picked up steam, many states permitted school systems to employ liberal arts college graduates who had never been in a preparatory program but who, after beginning to teach, would enter such a program. In New Haven the superintendent of schools visited campuses of elite colleges and universities to persuade seniors to consider teaching in New Haven, and he did hire a score or more of them.

We have no evidence that any of these efforts produced teachers who were superior to more conventionally trained ones. What I can say derives from my sustained experience with the teachers whom the superintendent attracted to New Haven. They were bright, highly motivated, aware they

---

3. I have discussed the conceptual and empirical flaws in these criticisms in previous books and cannot review them here in any detail. Needless to say, I am no opponent of brightness and subject matter, far from it. The point of the present book is that if teaching has artistic features and requirements, selection should take them into account.

were in above their heads, acknowledged they were not reaching many of their students, and did not feel they were getting the help they needed. That is based on weekly, 2-hour, group meetings I held with them over a 10-week span. I observed 10% of them in their classroom. By my criteria, and contrasting them with many more observations of new and conventionally trained teachers, they were neither better nor worse, which is to say that I was not impressed. Yes, in group meetings they impressed me as being more intellectually alive than conventionally trained teachers, but I saw no evidence of that liveliness in their classroom performance. If I have no evidence to say they were shortchanging their students, I have no evidence to say that their artistry turned students on. If one assumes they had a better grasp of subject matter in their specialty and other of the liberal arts, that grasp was not discernible by me.

What the critics of the time, and many critics today, have ignored is that the teacher is more than a mechanical conduit of information, but rather is a stage setter who seeks to get the actors to use themselves and their experience to make the substance of the script a part of their psychological bloodstream; the script has to become propelling, believable, personal, not a routinized, impersonal exercise the consequences of which enter the file-and-forget category of experience. The teacher is both stage director and performing artist, ever aware of how he or she might or should adapt to the obvious differences among the actors in their capacity to meet the requirements of their role. Those requirements are many and go beyond memory and recall, which are not to be confused with understanding. The word *under*standing makes the point: What is under or behind memory or recall? In what personal and intellectual contexts are they embedded? What self-motivating significances do they have? It is not enough that students can read the script, although that is not to be devalued. But beyond reading the script we expect the actor to have assimilated it so that its significances spread, again in terms of personal *and* intellectual meanings.

We take it for granted that it is the parental obligation to feed the very young child; to help the child learn to feed him- or herself, learn to stand upright, discriminate situations of physical danger, learn what is right and wrong; to toilet train the child; and more, much more. We may call it the parental script or curriculum. But does anyone deny that the script assumes—what the script will say and even plead for—that the parent is a sensitive, feeling, loving observer and responder, someone who tries to intuit and understand the child's overt behavior and messages, to adapt in ways that reinforce rather than weaken a child's dawning sense of competence and worth, to know the difference between empowering and indoctrinating, to distinguish between winning battles and losing wars? If we have learned anything in the past two centuries, it is that how parents set the stage and perform that script is a major determinant of how the very young child performs on that stage. Parents are told to sing to their very young child, to tell the child stories, to read to the child, to provide the child with toys that will elicit interest, to do damn near anything that elicits self-propelling curiosity, exploration, and wonder, which are the major "capital assets" making for productive learning.

Educational critics would agree with the above (I assume). What most critics ignore is that the script changes dramatically when the child begins "real" school. It is not only a change in the site and content of learning but in the theory of learning. I do not include here kindergartens because kindergarten and preschool teachers are in the culture of the "real" school not considered "real" teachers but more as sophisticated parents (or, as baby sitters, a put-down which these teachers resent). It is in the first grade that the change in the theory of learning is evident. The teacher has a calendar-driven, prescribed script-curriculum to which children must conform so that at the end of the year it can be demonstrated that the children have learned what the curriculum says they should have learned. It has long been the case that in the school culture time has become an implacable enemy of productive learning, an enemy that requires that the child learn by the clock or calendar. If only it was that simple, if only it was the case that young children did not vary widely in temperament, motivation, self-attitudes, anxieties, curiosity, etc. Are we to be smugly satisfied if at the end of first grade children are beginning to read? Satisfied, yes, but is it asking too much—an example of utopian expectations—to say that we hope these children *want* to read because reading for them has become a way of learning about self, others, and the world, not an activity intended only to satisfy adults? Is the goal of learning only to acquire content and skills, or is it also to acquire values and ways of thinking that pay off in terms of a self-propelling desire to know more, to learn that the more you know the more you want and need to know? We are all question-asking characters but never more so than when we were children. You would never know that from observing the modal American elementary classroom, even though in comparison to the modal middle and high school classroom, the elementary school almost comes up smelling roses.

If time is an enemy, the preparation of teachers conspires with that enemy to bulwark the status quo to an extent that critics vastly underestimate. Preparatory programs select, educate, and credential teachers who will know the curriculum far better than they know how to create and sustain some *semblance* of a context of productive learning despite the enemy of time, and that is because preparatory programs do not help students to understand and to perform in such a context. I should hasten to add that I have known teachers, albeit a small number, who, like Mr. Holland (*after* his initial totally self-defeating pedagogy), understand how of bedrock importance it is to take account of where the audience is coming from: to gear one's performance to make subject matter believable, meaningful, and connected to personal living and not an encapsulated oasis of knowledge and skills unconnected to personal feeling, relevance, and hopes. None of these teachers ever said to me that their cognitive and performance styles were a consequence of their formal training; some of them said it was despite that formal training. So, let me tell you about Mrs. Grillo.

For a number of years I collaborated with the late Dr. Burton Blatt in a preparatory program for teachers at Southern Connecticut State College (now university). There was a classroom for 8–10 students, one wall of which had one-way windows behind which we and program students would observe Mrs. Grillo and her class (Sarason, Davidson, & Blatt, 1987). Here is what we said to the observing students: "Each week during this semester we are going to observe this classroom. It is impossible to observe and not find yourself asking questions about individual children and what Mrs. Grillo does or does not do, when or why. After we have observed for an hour or so, we will return to the seminar room and discuss your questions." It was as short and as simple as that. We were totally unprepared for the near unanimous reluctance of the students to give voice to their questions. After some uncomfortable probing, two factors came to the surface. The first factor could be put this way: "We have never taught before or observed in a classroom. We don't know what questions to ask. We don't know what is important and what is not. Who are we to judge?" When, initially, we pointed out to them they were not ciphers in matters educational, that they had spent 12 years in classrooms, their reluctance diminished somewhat but over the course of the seminar that reluctance was never absent. I shall return to this factor later.

The second factor was Mrs. Grillo. She had the opposite of a soft voice; she could laugh at herself and students; she was personally revealing of what she thought and felt and why; she used different ways with different children to get them to talk about themselves, their friends, and their families; she was quick to discern when something was amiss in a student and use the occasion for group discussion (and solidarity); she was accessible to any student and no student hesitated to approach her for any reason; she was the epitome of spontaneity; she was always in motion, she rarely sat down; she was always scanning the scene; she was ebullient, inquiring, and one might say inquisitive; no student was in doubt that Mrs. Grillo was interested in and knew them. She knew she was a performer; she would quickly admit she was a "ham." Of course, her students loved her, put out effort for her, and learned a great deal, just as her display of love was believable to her audience.

The student observers were mammothly intimidated by Mrs. Grillo. As one of them said, "If that is what it takes to be a good teacher, I'll never be a good teacher." That was the consensus. In their 12 years as students in classrooms they had never seen a Mrs. Grillo, "who should have been an actress."

The image of a teacher these students possessed was someone who writes and directs a script the substance of which is important but impersonal and requires students to assimilate it in an equally impersonal way; that is to say, to leave it uncontaminated or interfered with by attitudes, feelings, or other "extraneous" factors. The student observers would say, of course, that a teacher should perform in a way so as to be seen as friendly and supportive. When asked what they meant by friendly and supportive, they would say the teachers should not have a punitive and demeaning manner, they should not play favorites, they should be patient and fair, they should be aware of and be able to give help to individuals who need it, they should create and sustain a relaxed ambiance that makes learning the script possible. Did not, we would ask, Mrs. Grillo meet these criteria? The students would be momentarily nonplused and then what would emerge is how impressed they were with (1) Mrs. Grillo's ebullience, spontaneity, and personal revealingness, (2) the personal spontaneity and expressiveness of the children, (3) the degree and intimacy between Mrs. Grillo and her students, and (4) how hard she and her students worked. The student observers could not see themselves "acting" like her.

Another factor at play is what may be called a concept of boundaries. In the case of the teacher that means there is a boundary, a clearly demarcated one, between personal experience and the substance and style of the teacher in the classroom. Mrs. Grillo used personal experience in no way as a form of confessional, but rather as a way of indicating commonalities between her and her pupils, and no less and perhaps more important, as a way to make it easier for students to be more personally expressive. In the case of the pupil the boundary is between what one is *expected* to say and do in the classroom and what one thinks and feels about the script; the classroom is a place—in Roger Barker's term a behavior setting (Barker & Gump, 1964)—where the truly personal has little or no place. So, for example, the classroom is not a place where you ask a lot of questions but where you dutifully appear to be motivated and paying attention, you understand, the script makes sense, you look forward to learning more, even though you cannot wait for the class and lesson to be over or for the school day to end. (Anyone who doubts this should talk to middle and high school teachers or, better yet, systematically observe their classrooms.) For Mrs. Grillo and her students the boundaries were porous, and not indiscriminately so.

As has been pointed out many times by many people, teachers teach the way they were taught. Their imagery of teachers and classrooms is highly overlearned. In fact, it is not unjustified to speculate that those who seek to become teachers are those for whom the conventional imagery of teachers and classrooms is congruent with their temperament, personal style, and capacity to "perform." That speculation, however, does *not* assume that those who seek to become a teacher must or should be a Mrs. Grillo. I have seen teachers, admittedly few in number, who on the surface are different than Mrs. Grillo but who in their distinctively different ways create and sustain an ambiance and relationships as she does. The Mrs. Grillos of this world are few. In the performing arts there are those who in this or that role are considered the standard by which all others are to be judged; it does not follow that all those who do not meet that standard should be, so to speak, excommunicated. It is one thing to fall somewhat below that standard, it is quite another thing to fall so far below it as to justify excommunication. The problem in education is that too many teachers fall far short as performers who can energize the intellectual and personal qualities and assets of their students. I may be guilty here of blaming the victim because not only do preparatory programs not select in appropriate ways by appropriate criteria but those programs are hardly, if at all (and I would say not at all), based on other than the most superficial conception of a teacher as a performing artist. They rivet so on subject matter and formula-like pedagogical techniques as to produce technicians, not the performing artists teachers should be.

The gist of most of what I have said was adumbrated by William James more than 100 years ago in his *Talks to Teachers on Psychology: And to Students on Some of Life's Ideals* (1902). The following is from the preface:

> In 1892 I was asked by the Harvard Corporation to give a few public lectures on psychology to the Cambridge teachers. The talks now printed form the substance of that course, which has since then been delivered at various places to various teacher-audiences. I have found by experience that what my hearers seem least to relish is analytical technicality, and what they most care for is concrete practical application. So I have gradually weeded out the former, and left the latter unreduced; and now, that I have at last written out the lectures, they contain a minimum of what is deemed "scientific" in psychology, and are practical and popular in the extreme.
>
> Some of my colleagues may possibly shake their heads at this; but in taking my cue from what has seemed to me to be the feeling of the audiences I believe that I am shaping my book so as to satisfy the more genuine public need.
>
> Teachers, of course, will miss the minute divisions, subdivisions, and definitions, the lettered and numbered headings, the variations of type, and

all the other mechanical artifices on which they are accustomed to prop their minds. But my main desire has been to make them conceive, and, if possible, reproduce sympathetically in their imagination, the mental life of their pupil as the sort of active unity which he himself feels it to be. *He* doesn't chop himself into distinct processes and compartments; and it would have frustrated this deeper purpose of my book to make it look, when printed, like a Baedeker's handbook of travel or a text-book of arithmetic. So far as books printed like this book force the fluidity of the facts upon the young teacher's attention, so far I am sure they tend to do his intellect a service, even though they may leave unsatisfied a craving (not altogether without its legitimate grounds) for more nomenclature, head-lines, and subdivisions. (p. III)

It is noteworthy that James felt obliged to start with where the audience of teachers were coming from: What they hoped for, needed, and wanted. I could, James says, trot out for this audience what psychology is as science, method, and content, but that will not talk to their practical problems in teaching children. Those practical problems will be small or large depending on how well teachers understand and respect how children think and feel. It is as if James is saying that the understanding and respect he has for where his audience of teachers is coming from is precisely how teachers should approach their students. If you do not know the minds and hearts of learners, thereby "hooking" them, you subvert productive learning. That is not for James a permissiveness, or indulgence, or a mindless obligation of leadership. It is the starting point, as the following quote indicates.

The native interests of children lie altogether in the sphere of sensation. Novel things to look at or novel sounds to hear, especially when they involve the spectacle of action of a violent sort, will always divert the attention from abstract conceptions of objects verbally taken in. The grimace that Johnny is making, the spitballs that Tommy is ready to throw, the dog-fight in the street, or the distant firebells ringing,—these are the rivals with which the teacher's powers of being interesting have incessantly to cope. The child will always attend more to what a teacher does than to what the same teacher says. During the performance of experiments or while the teacher is drawing on the blackboard, the children are tranquil and absorbed. I have seen a roomful of college students suddenly become perfectly still, to look at their professor of physics tie a piece of string around a stick which he was going to use in an experiment, but immediately grow restless when he began to explain the experiment. A lady told me that one day, during a lesson, she was delighted at having captured so completely the attention of one of her young charges. He did not remove his eyes from her face; but he said to her after the lesson was over, "I looked at you all the time, and your upper jaw did not move once!" That was the only fact that he had taken in.

Living things, then, moving things, or things that savor of danger or of blood, that have a dramatic quality,—these are the objects natively interesting to childhood, to the exclusion of almost everything else; and the teacher of young children, until more artificial interests have grown up, will keep in touch with her pupils by constant appeal to such matters as these. Instruction must be carried on objectively, experimentally, anecdotally. The blackboard-drawing and story-telling must constantly come in. But of course these methods cover only the first steps, and carry one but a little way.

Can we now formulate any general principle by which the later and more artificial interests connect themselves with these early ones that the child brings with him to the school?

Fortunately, we can: there is a very simple law that relates the acquired and the native interests with each other.

Any object not interesting in itself may become interesting through becoming associated with an object in which an interest already exists. The two associated objects grow, as it were, together: the interesting portion sheds its quality over the whole; and thus things not interesting in their own right borrow an interest which becomes as real and as strong as that of any natively interesting thing. The odd circumstance is that the borrowing does not impoverish the source, the objects taken together being more interesting, perhaps, than the originally interesting portion was by itself.

This is one of the most striking proofs of the range of application of the principle of association of ideas in psychology. An idea will infect another with its own emotional interest when they have become both associated together into any sort of a mental total. As there is no limit to the various associations into which an interesting idea may enter, one sees in how many ways an interest may be derived.

You will understand this abstract statement easily if I take the most frequent of concrete examples,—the interest which things borrow from their connection with our own personal welfare. The most natively interesting object to a man is his own personal self and its fortunes. We accordingly see that the moment a thing becomes connected with the fortunes of the self, it forthwith becomes an interesting thing. Lend the child his books, pencils, and other apparatus: then give them to him, make them his own, and notice the new light with which they instantly shine in his eyes. He takes a new kind of care of them altogether. In mature life, all the drudgery of a man's business or profession, intolerable in itself, is shot through with engrossing significance because he knows it to be associated with his personal fortunes. What more deadly uninteresting object can there be than a railroad time-table? Yet where will you find a more interesting object if you are going on a journey, and by its means can find your train? At such times the time-table will absorb a man's entire attention, its interest being borrowed solely from its relation to his personal life. *From all these facts there emerges a very simple abstract programme for the teacher to follow in keeping the attention of the child: Begin with the line of his native interests, and offer him objects that have some immediate con-*

nection with these. The kindergarten methods, the object-teaching routine, the blackboard and manual-training work,—all recognize this feature. Schools in which these methods preponderate are schools where discipline is easy, and where the voice of the master claiming order and attention in threatening tones need never be heard.

Next, step by step, connect with these first objects and experiences the later objects and ideas which you wish to instill. Associate the new with the old in some natural and telling way, so that the interest, being shed along from point to point, finally suffuses the entire system of objects of thought.

This is the abstract statement; and, abstractly, nothing can be easier to understand. It is in the fulfillment of the rule that the difficulty lies; for the difference between an interesting and a tedious teacher consists in little more than the inventiveness by which the one is able to mediate these associations and connections, and in the dullness in discovering such transitions which the other shows. One teacher's mind will fairly coruscate with points of connection between the new lesson and the circumstances of the children's other experience. Anecdotes and reminiscences will abound in her talk; and the shuttle of interest will shoot backward and forward, weaving the new and the old together in a lively and entertaining way. Another teacher has no such inventive fertility, and his lesson will always be a dead and heavy thing. This is the psychological meaning of the Herbartian principle of "preparation" for each lesson, and of correlating the new with the old. It is the psychological meaning of that whole method of concentration in studies of which you have been recently hearing so much. When the geography and English and history and arithmetic simultaneously make cross-references to one another, you get an interesting set of processes all along the line.

If, then, you wish to insure the interest of your pupils, there is only one way to do it; and that is to make certain that they have something in their minds *to attend with*, when you begin to talk. That something can consist in nothing but a previous lot of ideas already interesting in themselves, and of such a nature that the incoming novel objects which you present can dovetail into them and form with them some kind of a logically associated or systematic whole. Fortunately, almost any kind of a connection is sufficient to carry the interest along. (p. 92)

It should be obvious why I brought James into this discussion. I wish only to underline that in his contrast between the inventive and the dull teacher James was putting his finger on the teacher not only as a thinker but as a performing artist: "Anecdotes and reminiscences will abound in her talk; and the shuttle of interest will shoot backward and forward, weaving the new and the old together in a lively, entertaining way." (Why, when he describes the dull, non-inventive teacher, does he use the male pronoun?)

We can no longer afford to admit individuals to preparatory programs without some form of audition which will give us some basis for assessing how they interact with individual and groups of children in situations calling for inventiveness, spontaneity, and sensitivity. Devising such auditions and reliable ways of assessing them will be no easy job, and it will take time to determine in what ways these initial efforts should be revised. I am not suggesting that these initial efforts should even be used to accept or reject a candidate but rather that we begin the process of learning whether the judgments made by the conventional criteria now employed can be improved by auditions. It took years to develop an effective polio vaccine, and it will take years to achieve a way to distinguish between those who will become inventive or dull teachers. That will not sit well with reformers and political leaders who have two characteristics: an addiction to the quick fix and a capacity to oversimplify the educational system and its seemingly intractability to change. I should hasten to add that the selection of teachers is by no means the only major problem in our educational system. *But it is a major problem, and to deny that is to indulge ignorance, to avoid accountability, and to continue to short change future generations of students and teachers.*

In the next chapter I shall indicate the sources of my interest in auditions, an interest that goes back a long way although it is only in the past several years that I woke up to the fact that I had never given the issues the attention they deserved. I am now a very senior citizen in his eightieth year and in no position to act on the suggestions I shall offer in the next chapter. I console myself with the thought that what we need now is not a flight into action but a marketplace of ideas which will stimulate not only action but will elicit ideas more imaginative than what I have to offer. I write these words at a time when over the next 5–10 years a very large number of teachers will leave teaching. In addition, in some states (e.g., California) legislation has been passed to noticeably reduce class size. Those two facts, it has been argued, will make for a severe shortage of teachers. It may well be that it will produce a much larger pool from which to select teachers than has been the case since the decade and a half after World War II. As things are now, the selection will be no better than it was then. Even if the reader disagrees with anything or everything in this book, I would hope that is not because he or she thinks that issues of selection are unimportant, or trivial, and a waste of time.

CHAPTER 9

The Problematic Place of Theory
in the Preparation of Teachers

In the educational preparation of anyone who will directly interact with and influence the lives of others, what is or should be the relation between theory and practice?[1] The answer to that question was obvious to me (and everyone else) during the 20 years after World War II when I was director of Yale's graduate-doctoral program in clinical psychology. The field of modern clinical psychology was shaped by the Boulder Conference on clinical training over a 3-week period at Estes Park in Colorado, as reported in Raimy (1950). When you read that publication, several things are crystal clear. First, before a student meets his or her first patient that student should be well grounded in psychological-personality theory, the empirical origins and substances of the theories, research methods for assessing theory and practice, as well as courses intended to illuminate how clinical phenomena are related to other areas of psychology such as psychophysiology, human learning, social psychology, etc. It was expected that such preparation would be completed over a 2-year period after which the student would be placed in a clinical setting where, under supervision, the complexities and tools of practice would begin to be experienced and learned. It was not much different from medical school education: 2 years of basic courses followed by clerkships and internships.

I never questioned that rationale; it seemed so obviously correct and ethical. How could one justify "plunging" a wet-behind-the-ears student into a clinical interaction with a real, live patient without prior experience to theory? It took me many years to recognize some other "obvious" things. The first was that by the end of the second year of "basic" preparation stu-

---

1. After this book was in production I read an article in the *Harvard Education Review* by Thomas (1997) titled "What's the Use of Theory?" That article in very similar in theme to that of this chapter. The reader should consult that article.

dents could talk at length about theory and practice even though they were uttering abstractions hardly if at all grounded in personal experience. The second was that the students knew in an inchoate way, tinged with anxiety, that the moment of truth would be when they would start seeing patients; they knew that they knew theory but they were far from being secure that they knew how to apply theory appropriately. The third was that when they did start clinical work they saw the patients and themselves through the prism of theory, rendering themselves insensitive to what was going on in the here and now between them and their patients. It is not much of an exaggeration to say that they approached the clinical situation the way some people use recipes from a cookbook: you do A, then B, then C, etc., and voilá you have the desired dish, except that it does not have the expected taste. That you have to vigilantly watch what is going on, that you have to exercise personal judgment, that you should not ignore your intuitive feelings that something is awry, that the person who wrote the recipe took for granted what novices do not take for granted, that the artistry of the novice is not that of the recipe's writer—these considerations were not in the ken of the clinical students as they are not in the ken of the novice cook. The novice cook does not have to eat or serve a failed dish, but the clinical students knew they could not throw away the patient; they had an obligation they had to discharge in a helpful way, even though the psychological recipe does not provide a ready answer.

There was a final "obvious" factor to which I was insensitive and, therefore, was unable to question the theory-practice dichotomy: when I observed students in their clinical interactions, it was clear that students differed dramatically in their capacity either to unlearn psychological recipes and/or to adapt their personal style and words to individual differences among patients. Put in another way, although I concluded that some students were not cut out to be clinicians, I felt that having admitted them to the program, and the fact that for 2 years they had done well in their course work—usually doing very well indeed—we had a responsibility to work with them as best we could. In an entering cohort of eight clinical students there would be an average of two or three students about whom we had reservations in regard to their adequacy in a career in clinical psychology. That is an uncomfortably high percentage.

There was irony here which I failed at the time to note. The Yale department gave extra weight to an applicant for whom there was evidence in letters of recommendation that he or she had already engaged in research activity. The department deservedly took pride in the number of its students who later had outstanding research careers. In fact, each incoming student chose or was assigned to a faculty member with whom he was to work from day one; if you wanted to be a researcher, you did not have to wait until you finished courses in statistics or research design; you plunged into research under close supervision. The irony continued to escape me even after a report was published based on the deliberations of a very eminent group of researchers about research training in psychology (Garner, Hunt, & Taylor, 1959). Three of their major conclusions were (1) it was not sufficient to read about research, (2) you learned by doing, and (3) the picture you get of research from reading the literature is very misleading because it conveys the impression that the researcher is coldly objective, rational, nonintuitive, someone who always is secure in what he does and why, which is not the case at all. There is no direct line between theory and research design, between theory and analysis, between theory and choice of question to be researched. You learn about research and yourself by doing research; there is no cookbook that eliminates the researcher as observer, interpreter, reflector, and more. But if you learn about the nitty gritty of research by doing it from day one, how do you justify requiring clinical students to take 2 years of "basic" courses before they enter the clinical situation? It took me a long time to begin to ask the question, let alone to deal with it. By that time I was ready to step down as director of the program and turn to the arena of education.

Another irony. I said earlier that the Boulder Conference shaped modern clinical psychology. At that conference, which I attended, this question arose: Should we require clinical students to experience what it is like to be a patient with psychological problems? Would not such an experience make the clinician-to-be more sensitive and effective with the patients he or she would encounter? All people, it was said (correctly), have areas of personal insecurity, self-defeating behavior, and personal derogation, which may be small or large, areas which may be encapsulated or bounded or porous. Would not the experience of being a patient give a person a degree of self-understanding helpful for understanding others? In the abstract no one at the conference answered the question in the negative. What bothered them was that such a requirement would be an unfair, perhaps even unethical, economic burden on students, a display of authoritarian power that could have counterproductive consequences. We went on to other things. But no one saw any relationship between the suggestion and a rationale for the first 2 years of graduate school during which self-understanding, or how one uses one's self to help others, is not in the picture.

Several years before I retired, my late wife and I offered a case conference seminar for all first-year clinical students. The seminar had two goals: to learn how to conduct an intake interview and why, and to take on at least one patient in psychotherapy. The first goal did not meet any opposition from my colleagues. The second did on the grounds that these students lacked the personal, professional, and minimal knowledge to assume the role of psychotherapist. Besides, the time required of the students might take time away from the research project each first year student had to begin. My response had two interrelated parts. The clients would be carefully selected, and my late wife and I would provide at least one hour of supervision for each therapy session (based on tape-recorded interviews). The second part of my answer was that if we expect students to do research on clinical problems, should they not early on begin to experience the clinical situation and not only read about it?

We proceeded not because we were absolutely sure that we would not encounter difficult problems, although I would be less than honest if I did not say we were secure in the feeling that we could handle such problems and avoid harm to clients. The fact is that in the course of the seminars the students performed admirably and effectively, with two exceptions. The first exception was a young man who, beginning in the first supervisory hour, seemed intent on going his own way and ignoring any suggestions put to him. Finally, on the tape of one therapy hour the client asked him, "Do you think I am stupid?" To which the student replied, "Yes, I do." We recommended he not be allowed to remain in the clinical part of the graduate program, a recommendation my clinical colleagues did not accept. A year and a half later the student left Yale without explanation, and if credence is given to the student rumor mill, he was a very disturbed, hostile, sexually preoccupied individual. The second exception was a highly motivated, highly dependent, personally insecure, and self-castigating young lady who did not resist (indeed seemed to welcome) our advice to specialize in another area. In light of her overall course record, a year later the department terminated her. Aside from these two exceptions the students varied in their clinical performance—taking into account that they were beginners—from those showing promise as clinicians to three or four whose interpersonal sensitivity and style were remarkable.

How did we prepare the students for their initial encounter? Here is what we discussed with each student:

1. *Their conception of what takes place in a clinical interaction.* Where does that conception come from? In what ways is being helpful to a client similar to and different from being helpful to a friend? When are you forthcoming, and when are you not? What makes for a trusting relationship?
2. *Their anxiety and trepidation about seeing their first client.* How will you introduce yourself and why? Will you indicate you have read the intake interview (usually conducted by another student)? Will you, should you, ask why the person is seeking help now and not 6 or more months ago? Why might that be important?

3. *Their criteria for asking questions.* What criteria should determine when you ask what kind of a question? When should you feel free to say that you do not understand something the client has said? When are you justified in offering an interpretation, especially in the first hour? Do you offer it as proof of your clinical sophistication (!) or in the form of a question that allows the person to agree, disagree, elaborate, or ask you a question? What are the ways one thinks about silences. and when and how to deal with and utilize them? What is a "mistake" in psychotherapy? When and how do you own up to it, and what is the role of humor in a clinical interaction?

4. *Their initial need to follow a script.* Initially, at least, you will feel under pressure to "act" a role, a pressure that can or will cause you to be insensitive to the nuances of the substance of what the client does and says. Inevitably, you have a script, you will feel you need a script, to give justification and direction to the hour. That is not inherently wrong—it certainly is understandable—but you will over time learn that scripts when slavishly followed interfere with your understanding of what a client needs, thinks, and feels about being in therapy with you. The most active, positive ingredient in psychotherapy is when you and the client feel, without having to put it into words, relaxed and comfortable with each other, that you understand each other, that neither of you is "acting."

The main point of the above is to indicate that the student and supervisor will, over a period of weeks or months, be engaged in a conversation of how the "psychology" of the therapist will be of practical help to a person with personal, misery-producing behavior always invoking shame and guilt that have to be overcome if that behavior is to be put into words, faced, and discussed. And, no less important, that the relation between student and supervisor is both similar to and different from the relation between student and client.

We did not discuss theory. We discussed a student and client who are strangers to each other but who (usually on the next day) will be performing on the same stage, each of whom wants to be believable to and understood by the other. "Believable and understandable" are goals, they are not givens; they have to be won, and it requires that both change in some way. Psychotherapy is not a cookbook process; it is a developmental one which, the student is assured, will take more than a few years of practice to experience the difference between acting and performing a role.

What does this long introduction have to do with the selection of teachers? One reason, of course, is to argue that requiring courses in theory, methods, and even subject matter before exposure to practice with the kinds of people a teacher will confront is not as persuasively, self-evidently valid as is ordinarily claimed, *especially if a program takes seriously the obligation to select those whose personal style and qualities suggest the potential for spontaneity, inventiveness, personal expressiveness, and teachability.* Knowledge of subject matter is far from highly correlated with these characteristics. I am not claiming that knowledge of theory and subject matter are of secondary importance in professional growth and understanding of self and others but rather that they poorly compensate for the lack of the personal characteristics I listed above. (A personal example: Between the ages of 9 and 13 I took piano lessons from a conservatory-trained man who always determined what pieces I would play, never explained why those pieces and not others, was deadly serious, never asked me what I thought or felt about the music, let alone the kind of music in which I was interested; he never smiled, and he would proudly demonstrate how the pieces should be played, totally unaware that at the same time I was obviously impressed with his skill and artistry, I was concluding that I would never be a pianist. I was right. He never said anything to suggest that playing music required more than reading notes, striking the right keys and chords, and giving the appearance that you liked and understood the music.)

A second reason has to do with the role of auditions. What I mean by audition is illustrated by a suggestion I made to the New Haven school system when they sought to remedy a shortage of teachers by attracting graduating seniors from liberal arts colleges and universities who had no formal preparation whatsoever in teaching. My suggestion at that time was that a classroom with one-way windows and appropriate audio reception be used to observe each job applicant for one day with a group of students. The person would *not* be asked to "teach," or be given a specific educational script or goal, but rather to structure the day in whatever ways would be mutually interesting and rewarding for the students and the applicant. The applicant would have been told about this on a prior occasion. My suggestion received short shrift, which did not surprise me.

My suggestion, of course, begs several questions. What makes me think that the personality, stylistic, and temperament characteristics I listed are the crucial ones? The answer is twofold. The first is that those characteristics derive from observations of and relationships with many scores of teachers who ranged from what I and others regarded as inferior or mediocre to those it was a joy to watch, judgments which *seemed* to be those of their students as well. The second is that I readily admit that there may be other characteristics which are important. But we will never know that unless we begin seriously to undertake research programs to validate (or invalidate) our preconceptions and the kind of conventional wisdom which too frequently is conventional but not wise.

My list of characteristics is by no means intended as a complete one. For example, among teachers I have considered more than good, humor was a very frequent characteristic although humor, like any other characteristic, can be manifested in different ways in different people. Leon Lederman, a Nobel Laureate in physics, has in recent decades turned his attention to the preparation of science teachers. In the *New York Times* of July 14, 1998, he was interviewed by Claudia Dreifus. Here is a very brief excerpt from that interview.

> Q. You've been called "the Mel Brooks of the physics world." Brooks's humor is rooted in fear—fear of poverty, fear of the Holocaust. Where does yours come from?
> A. It comes from a terror of taking myself seriously. . . . It also puts me into a comfortable relationship with other people. It's human to want to make people laugh. It's part of teaching. Teaching is show business. Once, I gave a talk before the New York Science Teachers Association and we met at the Stardust Room at the Nevele Hotel (in the Catskills). And I knew all about that place from my childhood, from listening to the great comics like Zero Mostel who broadcast from there. And I was so thrilled to be there that I actually took the microphone off the stand and started telling jokes: "The teacher says to the student, 'Hey, wake up that kid sleeping next to you,' and the student says, 'Why should I? You put him to sleep!'"

I also recommend that interview to the reader for what Lederman says about the reaction of science teachers to a challenge of the usual order in which the sciences are taught. When asked what he has learned in his effort to improve the teaching of science, Lederman replied that the resistance to change is "awesome." Why he expected it would be otherwise reflects a naivete no less a feature of the thinking of reformers who grew up professionally in schools (Sarason, 1996b). Freud's intellectual legacy has been a mixed bag, but it is to his everlasting credit that he emphasized that resistance to change is one of the most predictable characteristics of people (Sarason, 1994).

I have never spoken to school administrators responsible for hiring teachers who denied that they wished their selections were far better than they were. And they all said that their decisions would frequently have been different if they had had the opportunity to observe applicants perform. I can paraphrase what many of them said in this way: "I interview the applicant with several questions in mind. Do I get a favorable impression? Do they strike me as friendly, relaxed, secure, or are they saying what they think I want to hear? Will they fit in with the other teachers, be a team player, or will they be the loner type? Where do they stand on discipline and working with parents? What problems have they had that they would like to avoid in this school? What do they consider their strong points? Why are they seeking a change? What questions do they put to me? Will I be able to work with them? Are they going to be hard to be with interpersonally? I have to be realistic. There may be only a handful of applicants, and I need a teacher. I have to choose from what I get. If I am replacing an experienced teacher, will the system allow me to hire another experienced teacher, assuming one is available, or must I make do with a novice or someone with far less of a teaching background in which case I know I am guessing? The longer I have been in this position, the more I feel it is all a crapshoot. I may appear confident in my choice, but most of the time I feel otherwise. I pray." I cannot refrain from saying what one administrator said: "Hiring a teacher is like getting married. You live with the person and then you find out what you wished you knew before. The rate of divorce in no way surprises me."

Candor requires that I say that I did not regard a fair number of these administrators as individuals with whose judgments—or the criteria they employed—I would be in agreement. That is to say, among those applicants they judged negatively, there might be some I might have judged otherwise, and similarly for those they judged positively, assuming that I employed the same interview process they did. And that is the point: Absent any opportunity to observe performance there is no way to resolve or learn from differences in judgment. When you seek to predict from one type of situation (interview) to an obviously different and more complex one (observing performance in a classroom), the room for error is considerable.

The second question begged by my list of characteristics is: Why do I think they can be reliably judged? That is to say, would different observers of performance rate those characteristics in the same or similar ways? Admittedly, those characteristics are neither easy to define nor to observe; their behavioral manifestations lack the specificity of eye color, weight, or height. But that is why you do research: to determine where the problems are, to engage in a self-correcting, self-improving process. The initial question is not my list, or an expanded one, but is whether any item on any list predicts a teacher's performance better than can be done with the present process. And, it bears repetition, the level of satisfaction with the present process is very low.

The third question begged by my list is that I seem to be describing a teacher who is a paragon of personal virtues. Spontaneity, inventiveness, personal expressiveness, flexibility-teachability—how many people have all of these and similar characteristics? The answer, of course, is not many. Accepting that fact, the task is to determine how much any one characteristic contributes to predictions about who becomes a good, bad, or average teacher, or which combination of any two improves prediction.

Regardless of your or my choice of characteristics, their appropriateness or usefulness is not persuasive unless you can demonstrate that they contribute to prediction. You or I may find our choices persuasive but personal opinion is just that: personal, subjective, and subject to the frailties of human judgment. At the present time we may not be flying blind, but a very good case could be made that we are flying in the clouds without instruments.

Opera requires singers who can sing *and* act. The history of opera is replete with examples of individuals who could hardly act but who had glorious voices, or who had less than glorious voices but were superb actors, or who were just average in voice and acting. Audiences and opera teachers would like performers to be equally gifted as singers and actors but, far more often than not, they have to decide whether the quality level of one characteristic compensates for a higher or lower quality level in another characteristic. Over the decades I have directly observed very few teachers who were high on all or even most quality characteristics—such teachers are and will always be rare. But I have seen more teachers who were low on some characteristics but high on one or two, high enough for me to conclude that I would be satisfied if my child was in their classrooms. Candor requires that I say that most teachers I observed over more than 4 decades were not discernibly high on any characteristic that would compensate for their low quality level on others. I am not "blaming" these teachers because to do so would be a case of blaming the victim. There are no villains here. There is a system guaranteed to short change those who seek to be teachers and a school culture that adds insult to injury.

The problem I have raised is, in my opinion, initially not a research issue but a moral one, by which I mean that the selection of teachers is too societally important to be conducted as it now is. When there is universal agreement that (1) teachers are of bedrock importance in the education of students and (2) the general quality of teaching today satisfies nobody (including most students), it is immoral that so little is being done that goes beyond token gestures (if that). I emphasize the moral because the research problem is, to indulge understatement, a daunting one that will take years before we will know what we need to know, before we can demonstrate that new procedures and ways of thinking are better than we now have, which is to say that they are better than tossing a coin. That kind of research will be neither easy nor cheap; like most research, there will be failures, potholes, and cul-de-sacs. But unless that research does not emerge from a context of moral outrage and a heretofore-absent political courage and leadership—the opposite of the self-defeating quick-fix mentality rooted in ignorance so characteristic of the political establishment—the problem will remain as it is, or get worse.

It is obvious from this and previous chapters that I believe that the selection process has to include in a major way direct observation of the candidate in a situation similar to but not necessarily identical with the classroom one. I can assure the reader that I know that it is easier said than done. When you seek to predict behavior in x situation from data in y situation, should not y be of a kind that allows the characteristics you have deemed important to be manifested? I am not opposed to interviews and psychological tests—they have their place—but when they are the sole basis for selection, they are and have been found wanting. Let me illustrate this with an example.

A dear friend of mine is Professor Robert Fried of Northeastern University in Boston. He is the author of *The Passionate Teacher* (1995), which I recommended in Chapter 5 as a superb book containing descriptions of good teachers and teaching. The book came to the attention of an executive of an association of schools for American children whose parents work in Europe, the Mideast, and South East Asia. The number of these schools is not small. Once a year teachers from each of these schools come together to share experiences, identify issues and problems, and spend several days interacting with an invited educator. At their meeting in Bangkok in 1998, Dr. Fried was the invited guest lecturer and seminar leader. It is also the practice that the teachers are asked to write an essay illustrative of a moving experience they had as a teacher. Special recognition and prizes are given to the three essays judged of excellent quality. What follows is one of the essays by a young woman currently teaching in Bombay, India. It is about her first teaching experience in Oakland, California. I give it in its entirety.

Alone on the Stage
(Reflections, Writing, and the Art of Teaching)
Laura Vaidya

Picture a boulevard lined by crumbling fifties-era apartment buildings. Liquor stores, with names like Jacks or Black & White, sit on every corner. Billboards of beautiful black models, pitching hair products or cigarettes look down from high. Check cashing outlets, small food stores, with "lotto," displayed in their dirty windows, nail shops, and seedy bars, Colt 45 Malt Liquor signs flashing above the doors, comprise the squalid retail mood of the street. Middle-aged men are assembled in small groups, some are sitting on broken bus benches, others are standing and sipping from bottles they tote inside brown paper bags. It is early morning. Police cruise by, suspiciously eyeing the well-dressed teenagers whose thick gold chains and heavy rings single them out as "dealers."

As you approach East 98th Ave. and MacArthur, the run-down shops give way to a block of decrepit tan buildings laid out in barrack-style, surrounded by gape-holed cyclone fences. CASTLEMONT HIGH SCHOOL is painted in red letters on the upper facade. The C, T and L have been painted out, leaving the name preferred by rival schools, "asemont High School." Three Oakland, California, squad cars are parked in front of the open gated entrance. Yellow grass and broken saplings decorate the narrow pathway leading to heavy front doors. They are closed. Guards, carrying walkie-talkies, open it to a white teacher wearing the mid-calf, Indian-cotton full skirt and turtleneck T-shirt that scream "Berkeley," and by association "liberal chump," to the students who are ambling in through a side-door entrance. The students, mostly black, are dressed in the latest styles of sagging pants for the boys, baggy jeans and short, belly-revealing tops for the girls. Everyone has on expensive athletic shoes or black-leather, military-style boots. Most of the girls wear elaborate hairstyles, some dyed orange and braided in hundreds of tiny rows, wound around their heads in intricate designs. The boys' hair is worn short or shaved. Most of the girls have long nails, painted in two- or three-tone colors and often decorated with gold sparkle or rhinestones. At least half of the students are overweight. Among this gathering can be seen an occasional Asian girl or boy, looking small and lost among their mostly bigger African-American schoolmates. A few Hispanic boys, wearing the uniform of their "barrios"—oversized work shirts buttoned to the top, enormous, baggy, black work pants cuffed several times and slicked back long hair—stride aggressively through the increasingly crowded hallways. Everyone moves out of the way.

The teacher walks cautiously along the halls looking for the main office. Surly, uncommunicative workers from other offices point the wrong way. She finally spots an elderly, bossy-looking woman directing students, and asks her for directions. The woman looks her up and down, a condescending smile plays at her lips. "Come with me," she says, as she leads the teacher along a maze of metal locker-lined corridors to yet another side office.

The teacher walks in and announces her status to the secretary, a middle-aged black woman. The secretary surveys the new arrival, shaking her head. "You are the drama teacher replacement?" she asks, skepticism dripping from every word. "Has anyone told you about those classes?" The woman responds that her only information is that the former teacher had quit without notice after only three days. The secretary merely shakes her head. . . .

The above scene took place seven years ago in Oakland, California, home to one of the worst school systems in the United States. I was that teacher, who, at five-foot three, and a hundred and ten pounds, felt like a midget among the giant adolescents. By the time I'd reached that office, my already pounding heart was beginning to gyrate madly inside my chest. Nevertheless, I resisted the urge to bolt, so obediently took the class keys and student rosters. The secretary curtly informed me that the bell had rung and the students had been let into the class already. "So get up there immediately," she said.

As I proceeded towards the classroom, I spotted an attractive well-dressed African-American teacher from one of my children's former schools. "Mrs. Washington," I yelled, thrilled to see a familiar face.

"Why Mrs. Vaidya, what are you doing here?

"I just started teaching. This is my first day."

Mrs. Washington's smile faded. "Don't tell me you're the new Drama teacher," she said, a firm emphasis on the tell.

"Yes I am."

She grabbed my arm, squeezing hard. "Don't go in there. You're the second replacement they've hired. The last one quit after only one day." She leaned over and whispered, "The students hate white people."

By now my hands were visibly shaking and my knees were wobbling, but as much as I wanted to turn around and get out of there, I was determined to stay. I had become a teacher because I had the notion that I could make a difference and had accepted this position because I had wanted the challenge. I had thought love and good will could change even hardened students into good boys and girls. In other words, I'd read the wrong books and believed them.

I cautiously moved on up the stairs along the long, dull corridors to room 104. I hesitated at the door, but could hear nothing. I started to open it, lost my nerve, walked away, came back and pushed it open. The same "bossy" woman was inside. She looked at her watch, a gesture that made me acutely aware of my tardiness, hastily introduced me to the students, then pulled me outside to provide some "administrative support," as she was the assistant vice principal. "You must establish who is the boss immediately," she said, "or they won't respect you." With that wonderful advice, she left.

I went back in and looked around the room. It was amazingly ugly. Stained poster-board lined two sides of the cement walls, old-fashioned pull-up windows, facing the parking lot, covered the other wall. Behind me was a faded green-board and yellow chalk. The walls were bare, with not a hint of anything related to drama, English, students, even school. Empty bookshelves were laid out along the back wall and locked closets ran along the wall next to the door.

I looked over at the students. My roster indicated a classroom of thirty-six, but there were only about twenty-three. This is typical of such schools. On most days, half of the students don't show up. The ones that were in attendance mostly ignored me. Girls were chatting among themselves, applying makeup or eating noisily from bags of chips. Boys were pounding rap beats on desks, loudly calling back and forth to one another. A few students were wandering aimlessly among the graffiti-scarred desks.

It was a mixed-grade beginning drama class. Almost all of the students were black. One boy and two girls looked Hispanic. There was one Asian student, a boy who I later learned had just come from Mainland China and could speak almost no English. Two of the girls were visibly pregnant. I was later to learn that the youngest one, only fourteen years old, was having her second baby. Three or four students watched me with an open hostility that bordered on hatred. I later learned this is called "mean mugging."

I stood before them too frightened to speak. Finally I took a deep breath, held my shaking hands up before them so that they could see the tremors, and said. "Look at my hands, are you really as bad as everyone has told me? Because, I am terrified." There was a stunned silence. At least I'd gotten their attention.

Some of them began to murmur, "She's trippin'." There were a few hostile guffaws.

One boy got up, a huge kid, broadcasting a bad attitude. "Hey, hurry up and take the roll, I gotta go." Everyone laughed derisively.

I pulled out a sheet of paper, drew the seats on it and told them to sign their names. I said I'd make a seating chart from it. Amazingly they all placed their names in the appropriate spots.

The bad attitude boy placed his name in a square then got up and began to saunter out. "I sit where I want to," he said. As he opened the door to leave, he warned, "You better not mark me absent you white bitch." The door slammed shut to the wild, high-pitched hysterical laughing of the other students. I looked at the clock. Only ten minutes had passed. Time wasn't dragging. It wasn't crawling. Time had ceased altogether.

I walked over to the green board and wrote my name. Under it I wrote "Love."

"Hey, you a hippie?" one kid yelled. I ignored him.

Someone else muttered, "She be straight-out fuckin' hippie." I ignored her too.

"I want you to write as fast as you can for ten minutes," I said. "Don't lift your hands from the paper. Don't think, just write. You can say anything you want, just make sure it begins with the word love."

"What's love got to do with this drama shit?" a skinny ninth grade boy said.

"Hey, this ain't supposed to be no writing class," another yelled.

I ignored them all. "I want you to begin at the count of three— one, two, three," I said, "begin." No one moved. "Would you please get out your pens and paper," I repeated. No one moved.

"Hey, Ms. Vaidya, we don't got no pens or paper," a girl said.

"You're the teacher you spose' to give it to us," another yelled.

I went to the teacher's desk to pull out some paper. There was none. In fact, there was nothing but a few clips, some blue passes and a few erasers.

A tall, handsome kid in the back, luckily a track star and popular, got out a pad and began to pass sheets of paper around. "You can use some of mine," he offered.

I was absurdly grateful. As soon as they got their paper, a few pencils began to materialize. I looked madly in the shelves and uncovered about ten more.

I told them a third time about the "timed writing" and miracle! They all began to scribble madly on their sheets. They wrote a lot of cliches about love. Mostly how God was love and only God's love was important. A few wrote descriptive accounts of physical love. PLEASE READ TO CLASS was written in bold letters on top of the papers. Damn, I thought, this approach to the topic had never occurred to me. (I was amazingly naive.) However, true to my promise, I read each and every one aloud, substituting the letter "F" for the four letters it denoted.

Not censoring their work earned me a few points, which translated into grudging cooperation. Interestingly, they soon tired of pornography and began to write more seriously. Each timed piece was better than its predecessor. I was amazed at how open they were. Horrible childhood memories, awful events like rape and murder were shared with enthusiasm. Criminal activities, such as dealing or prostitution, were especially regarded as great writing topics. They loved the attention of having their work acknowledged yet they wanted to be viewed as "hard."

While they wrote about life's underbelly with gusto, tenderness, kindness, enthusiasm for school and appreciation of beauty, were all forbidden topics. Kindness was the province of grandmothers and God. Beauty was for queers and nerds. Love was for hippie chumps, like their pathetic teacher, whom they slowly began to tolerate. Most of the students saw themselves as irredeemably "bad." Yet slowly, surely, the mood of the classes began to change. I was lucky. Having a few popular student leaders on my side was a great boost. It also helped that my eldest daughter, a cheerleader at Skyline High School, a school in the Oakland hills, was known by a few of the athletes. That earned me a few more crucial points. Also, Mr. Bad Attitude, who I quickly started thinking of as a thug, left after three days. He was too street tough even for these students and his illiterate essay about how much he loved killing animals with his "gat" (gun) earned him some boos. Had he stayed, I might not have made it.

Yet the deciding factor in my progress with the students was the use of timed writings. Somehow, I had accidentally grasped a technique for reaching their spirits. By the end of the first week, they were given slightly more complex subjects and were asked to stand up themselves to read aloud. From there, we turned their writing into "monologues," then chopped them up, created two speakers and made "dialogues." The kids were natural performers as surviving in the inner city required consummate acting skills. Being tough, being heartless and full of hatred were the required postures and they were always "on."

After about two weeks, the dialogues were put together into scenes. They were wonderfully inventive. One timed writing had inspired an imaginative skit titled "My Ghetto Dog," in which the kids took the parts of different street-smart, wise-cracking mutts. However, as good as the work became, one performance profoundly changed my life and was a turning point in my commitment to teaching.

There was a student in my class who had resisted all attempts at contact. He had refused to write or participate in any assignment. Yet he came faithfully to class each day and just as faithfully slept through the entire period. Almost two weeks into the course, I learned he was "emotionally disturbed," in Special Education, and was being "mainstreamed" illegally without the services of an aide. I could have had him removed, but I didn't. Instead, I decided to persuade him to participate. To my amazement, a little prodding resulted in success. He agreed to write a monologue on the condition that I record it and play it to the class while he was not present. I agreed. A few days later he presented me a poem. I said I'd meet him after school to record it. He didn't show up, so I assumed he had backed down. I was wrong. The next day he showed up in class. He said he'd changed his mind and was ready to perform his monologue in front of the class. I was skeptical and nervous for him and even tried to talk him out of it. I didn't want to see him humiliated. He was a mixed-race child, who would have been handsome had he not had such a slump-shouldered, depressed demeanor. He seemed totally friendless, almost invisible. When he took his place alone on the small, school stage to perform, many of the students began to snicker. I held my breath as he sat there silently, head bowed, clutching his wrinkled, messy work. Suddenly, he looked up, sat straight, gazing fixedly at the audience. In a strong, sure voice, he began to speak.

In the good old days there was a family.
They had a house and a yard.
A bike and wading pool sat on the grass.
Children laughed and had fun in the yard.

In the good old days there was a big kitchen.
A mother cooked fried chicken and greens.
She baked biscuits and pies,
Her family sat together at the kitchen table.

In the good old days there was a boy.
He played with his cousins.
They ran to the stream and threw stones at the fish,
They chased birds and ran with the dog.

In the good old days there was Christmas.
With a Christmas tree,
It was decorated with lights and bright balls.
There were presents under the tree.

In the good old days the children
Opened the presents
And sang Christmas songs.
There was a stocking for the dog.

Nowadays, the yard is overgrown.
Nowadays, the kitchen is empty.
Nowadays, the children don't play anymore.
Nowadays, there is no Christmas tree,
There are no presents.

Like smoke in the mist,
They are gone.
Like tears in the rain,
They are gone.
Like water flowing down a gutter into a void,
THEY ARE GONE.

And will never return.

I want to go back to the good old days.
I want to eat my mother's fried chicken.
I want to play in the yard and
Run with my cousins.

I want a Christmas tree and presents,
A family with a dog.

But I can't.
The good old days are gone.
The good old days are gone and will never come back.
How I wish I could go back to the good old days.
But I can't.

The boy finished his recitation, bowed his head and sat as silently as before. The class was so quiet you could hear birds chirping outside. Tears ran down my cheeks. I looked around and saw that many of the girls were also crying. The boys were mute. Then we began to clap. Students were cheering. The quiet boy stood up, bowed, then took his seat. I went over and embraced him. He hugged me back.

That was the finest moment of my teaching career. Since then I've had some fine moments, but nothing has ever rivaled the courage, beauty and humanity of that shy, abandoned child, baring his soul to us.

Were this fiction, the shy, outcast boy would have then gone on to make friends, get out of special education and begin to rebuild "the good old days." Sadly, that didn't happen. A few weeks later he disappeared. His caseworker told me he had been placed in a group home for mentally disturbed youth. Apparently some horrible trauma, she thought his father had murdered his mother, had placed him outside our sphere of succor. I never heard about him again. The caseworker quit, the school didn't follow his progress and I left Castlemont. I'd only been there three months and had no desire to return. My favorite students were graduating, the others were dropping out.

Looking back I know I made the right decision. My successes had been many, but my failures had been greater. However, I had made an important realization. The books I'd read were wrong; idealism and good intentions weren't enough, teaching also required courage, compassion, tenacity and indefatigability. Yet despite the often thankless nature of the work, I also knew I wanted to remain a teacher. A passion to seek and nurture the unexpressed, and, in many cases, the unrealized potential of students had been ignited. I was hooked.

AFTERWORD

I had been aware at the time of my experience that I had learned a great deal and grown from the encounter with the young man in the narrative. Yet, the process of writing it has been cathartic.

I've often been upset by my shortcomings as a teacher, thinking I could have given more, done more, given less or done less. Yet, working on this narrative provided the perspective of time and experience allowing me to realize that I had accomplished what I could at the time. Perhaps today I would have pursued the child more energetically and not let him slip away so easily, but, it was my first teaching job and I was uncertain of my options and of my potential as a teacher. In any case, I grew from the experience and writing about it has shown me just how valuable that growth has been.

The essay raises a host of questions some of which are speculative. What is not speculative (in my opinion) is that Ms. Vaidya is an unusual person and teacher. She is courageous, inventive, spontaneous, personally expressive, flexible, and reflective. The speculative question is: How was she regarded by those in the preparatory program who had recently credentialed her? She started in the position 3 months before the end of the school year when the previous teacher quit and left, without explanation or notice. Why was Ms. Vaidya available? Why was she unemployed? Was it that she had not been highly regarded by those in the preparatory program; that she came across in ways that did not engender confidence in her teaching abilities? How many school systems rejected her because of an interview and/or a poor recommendation from the preparatory program? Obviously, I have to ask these questions because (1) I regard her as a very unusual person, and (2) it is scandalous and immoral to place her or any other neophyte in the school she describes. That she performed as well as she did forces me to ask: Would her performance have surprised those who "trained" her and, if so, why? If I have no answers to these speculative questions, I feel justified in saying that until we obtain credible evidence about the relationship between how programs select and train their students and how those students perform as teachers, the quality of teaching in the modal classroom will not improve.

But in obtaining that credible evidence one of the most thorny and important problems in education will have to be confronted. How does the culture of our schools nurture and support the personal, professional, and intellectual development of teachers, especially in the early years of their careers? To what extent does that culture require a stultifying conformity and extinguish or mammothly constrain the characteristics displayed by Ms. Vaidya? In her Oakland school Ms. Vaidya was, so to speak, thrown to the wolves. No one was disposed to be supportive in the slightest degree. Granted that that school is an extreme case, but only somewhat less extreme cases are not at all rare in urban school systems. In *Mr. Holland's Opus* Mr. Holland was also "Alone on the Stage" in a white, suburban high school, unprepared for what he would confront, with no one to help or advise him, no one to unleash personal characteristics similar to those Ms. Vaidya displayed. He had to be hit over the head, so to speak, in his interaction with a student, to begin to realize why he had failed his students. And with that realization he was able to see and to give expression to characteristics he possessed but had not been in evidence as a teacher.

In recent years the literature on teachers and teaching has emphasized the importance of professional development and how crucial it is to avoid stagnation, routinization, resistance to learning and changing, and ultimately burnout. This ever-burgeoning literature is testimony to the recognition that the culture of schools is generally inimical to the growth of the teacher as a performer. We are used to hearing that the goal of teaching is to help each child "realize his or her full potential." That way of putting it may serve the purpose of sloganeering, but it masks the fact that the realities of the school culture make a mockery of that purpose. *The reasons are many and complex, but surely one of the reasons is that the school culture makes a mockery of the professional development of teachers* and matters are not helped any by preparatory programs whose criteria of the teacher as performing artist are so poor, thereby bulwarking the stultifying features of the culture of the school. Candor requires that I say from what I know and have read about programs for the professional development of teachers that they are almost always intellectual and informational in nature and hardly (if at all) focus in any direct way on how the teacher performs, how the teacher conceives of and discharges the performing artist's obligation to an audience of students. Teaching is an interpersonal affair, and as soon as you say "inter" you mean (or should mean) that teacher and student(s) *seek* to understand each other and it is in the process of seeking that the qualities of the teacher as performing artist can be observed.

It goes without saying that the performing artist knows the script (= subject matter), be it a teacher, a singer, pianist, actor, etc. But long before I ever came on the educational scene, there were those who stated the obvious: Between the script and the audience is a performing artist whose artistry determines to what extent the audience will be stimulated, moved, energized, and responsive, or unmoved, disinterested, bored, disappointed, disillusioned, eager that the occasion should end. No one disputes that in regard to the conventional performing arts; everyone regards that as a glimpse of the obvious. But when it comes to teaching as a performing art, it is another story, the central theme of which is that teachers convey information and demonstrate and supervise the acquisition of skills, both according to a predetermined sequence. And that theme is associated with imagery of dutiful students whose responsibility it is to listen, follow directions, do their homework, and work hard.[2] It is imagery of a classroom that recognizes little or not at all the artistry a teacher should have or the fact that each student has an individuality which if not recognized and nurtured makes the classroom a frustrating, boring place where what you feel and what questions you have are concealed in an unwanted privacy.

The day before these words were written I, together with five educators, watched videos of the teaching of geometry in three classrooms, one each from Japan, Germany, and the United States. The videos were made

---

2. Popular imagery of teachers and classrooms has a long history and diverse sources. That imagery goes a long way to explain why in the university schools of education are held in low repute. The university is based on the axiom that a solid grasp of subject matter is credential enough to teach that subject matter. Schools of education are based on an opposing axiom: Grasp of subject matter is not sufficient to ensure good teaching of subject matter. This derogation of schools of education reflects imagery of teachers and students that would be laughable if its consequences were not so pernicious. And what evidence do we have that university teachers are far superior on average to school teachers?

by the organization which conducts testing on an international basis to assess student performance. The recent report of the assessment was no source of satisfaction to American authorities. They were surprisingly (to me) very good videos because when each was finished we had a rather clear picture of what the teacher's goal was, how the two male teachers and one female teacher conducted the class, and student response. Three of the viewers were, to say the least, highly trained scientists (two from the United States, one from Israel) whose grasp of geometry is considerable. As soon as the videos were finished the three exclaimed that the level of difficulty of the geometry problem in the Japanese classroom was discernibly greater than in the German and American classroom. But what struck all of us with force was that in the Japanese classroom the teacher used humor; he had a relaxed, playful style, and would engage in a give-and-take with students who were no less relaxed or spontaneous in their comments and reactions, and who contributed their own brand of humor. This was in startling (I use that word advisedly) contrast to the German and American class-rooms. The female German teacher was, to indulge understatement, a phlegmatic, laid back, unimpressive individual who never displayed feel-ing. The American teacher was far more alive and obviously eager to cover his predetermined lesson plan. As for the American and German students I can only say that all of us described them as passive listeners who never asked a question or whose facial expressions never conveyed interest (let alone enthusiasm) or for that matter anything resembling motivation. The contrast between the Japanese classroom and the other two classrooms was stark. I mention these videos not for the purpose of substantiating my char-acterization of the modal American classroom but in order to remind the reader that as students go from elementary to middle to high school their interest in and motivation for learning (in schools, at least) decreases. I should hasten to add that those findings cannot be attributed only to the inadequacies of teachers, although to deny that these inadequacies play a major role is strange, unrealistic, and indefensible.

In this book I have argued that the selection, preparation, and profes-sional development of teachers require direct observation, not only tests, letters of recommendation, courses, workshops, and the like. That state-ment would be regarded as a glimpse of the obvious by those in the per-forming arts. It is the opposite of obvious in matters of teaching. The videos I discussed above are examples of what I mean.

I come now to the final question begged by what I have said. It is the most important question, and I devote the next chapter to it. Schooling has many purposes, but certainly they are not of equal importance. A colleague of mind, Dr. John Doris, once asked this question: If you had to choose between passing on to your children your genes or your values, which would you choose? I leave it to the reader to answer the question. In the next chapter I give my answer to the question: granted that schools have several very important purposes, is there an overarching purpose which, if not achieved, negatively affects achieving other purposes? How you answer that question is crucial for the selection, preparation, and professional development of teachers; unless, of course, you view teaching not as a performing art, but as a conduit for information and the learning of skills. That would be like saying that the task of the piano teacher is to ensure that the student can read notes, play them without error, and use the foot pedals as indicated, to the point where the student can play the piece from memory—all else is secondary. Such an achievement is not to be derogated if that was its sole, narrow purpose, but when that purpose is part of a combination of purposes for learning about music and piano playing, achieving that narrow purpose is not only narrow but may be counterproductive of related purposes (if any).

CHAPTER 10

The Overarching Goal and the Performing Teacher

What is or should be the overarching purpose of schooling? I shall endeavor to answer that question later in this chapter, but I shall preface that answer by discussing two questions: Why do people seek a career in the performing arts? What light does the women's liberation movement shed on who seeks a career in teaching?

As I said earlier in this book, those who seek formal training in the performing arts already have had varying degrees of direct experience (sometimes formal) in acting, or in music, or in the dance. They have had role models whom they have seen in live performance, on TV, and in the movies. And, by no means infrequently, they have read about them in the mass media and biographical accounts. This is by way of saying that these aspirants have acquired knowledge about what a career in the performing arts entails. I do not want to exaggerate the extent or validity or realism of their knowledge, but by the time they seek formal training they have a fair degree of understanding of the artistic culture which they seek to enter. What deserves emphasis is that among the major attractions of the career is that there will *always* be challenges and self-testing, diversity of roles, new learning. They do not see the career in static terms; built into expectations is a vision of a personal trajectory in which there is the combination of new learning and the soaking up of new experience. The would-be actor knows that the roles appropriate and available to him or her in their early years will change as the years go on. The singer knows that time is the enemy of voice. The dancer knows that time is the enemy of the body. But if time is the enemy, it is also the spur to continue to learn and do as much as one can to nourish the need to sustain the sense of growth. And these are careers where the obvious feature is that what the performer does is always public *and* judged by audience, teachers, and critics. Whatever the self-judgment of the performer, in a crucial sense "success" will depend on the judgment of others. Like it or not, the performer has to take life-long learning seriously. Self-improvement is the name of the game. Even when Arthur Rubenstein was well along in years and a world-renowned pianist, in response to criticisms of his playing, he took off one year to improve his accuracy, to rethink his interpretive style, and to practice, practice, practice. To be criticized for stagnating or "plateauing" is a mortal wound to the artist's sense of worthiness. To continue to learn and grow is the overarching goal.

Up until the 1960s those seeking a career in teaching were mostly women, although after World War II the number of men seeking to become teachers had steadily increased. Most of these women and men came from backgrounds which viewed teaching as a respectable, satisfying, secure career. Two factors began to change the outlook of these groups. The first arises from what may be called "the sizzling sixties" when every major societal institution came under attack, especially from young people. Schools were not exempt; indeed, they were at or very near the center of conflict because they contained or exhibited all the issues around equity, race, civil rights, and disappointing educational outcomes. Teachers and teaching were seen as part of the problem, not of the solution. Schools were not seen as places where students and teachers learned and grew. That was especially the case in conflict-ridden, urban areas. It was during that decade that many teachers and school administrators retired or left teaching. As more than a few said to me, "I've had it. I don't want to take it anymore." And it was not rare for me to be told, "I'm a teacher. My mother (or father) was a teacher, but I would not want my daughter (or son) to go into teaching."

It was also the decade of an emerging, growing, militant women's liberation movement, which at its core was a revolt against the view that the place of women was in the home or at a typewriter in an office or as a nurse or in any low paying, low level, non-creative, unchallenging role. The axiom undergirding the movement was: We are more, can do more, can become more than society has heretofore allowed. And precisely because teaching was one role to which society had consigned women—it was a variation on the theme of rearing the young—there were women who came to view teaching as no less than supportive of age-old discrimination. And, of course, matters were not helped any by the interaction of such a view with what was happening in that turbulent decade. Women were not only demanding equal access to an ever-increasing job market but to those parts of it they considered would be challenging over a lifetime. Being a teacher was not at or even near the top of their list; teachers were at the bottom of an institutional hierarchy that made the crucial decisions independent of the educational proletariat. And it was largely a hierarchy the upper levels of which were controlled by males.

In the case of men the story is different, but the underlying theme is very similar. It was during the sixties that math and physics teachers began to leave teaching and take positions in computer and allied fields. It was not only because they would be better remunerated but, no less important, they would be embarking on a new career which gave promise of novelty, challenge, and fulfillment over the course of that career. It was that kind of promise that in large part explains why the number of men who *sought* to become math, physics, science teachers dramatically began to dwindle; they saw teaching as a kind of dead end.

In 1977 I wrote *Work, Aging, and Social Change*. That book is about what I call the one-life, one-career imperative: At the point of deciding on a career, society says, so to speak, "You can be A, B, or C. You cannot be A *and* B, B *and* C, or A *and* C. You have to choose in which career you will be over the course of your working life." Before World War II that imperative seemed necessary, natural (obvious), and desirable. But as a consequence of the mammoth social change ushered in by World War II (Sarason, 1996a) —those changes manifested most clearly in the sixties—the one-life, one-career imperative engendered resistance in young people. They resented having to make a "final," life-shaping decision, they did not want to be "slotted" in large, impersonal organizations in which the sense of growth might wither, conformity was the rule, and creative challenges few and far between. I said earlier that the word *entrapment* (and its associated dysphoric imagery) is one heard frequently among young people. Even more frequent is the word *growth*, the intended meaning of which is, especially in regard to work and career, that with the passage of time one's individuality and need for challenge and a gratifying diversity of experience will be recognized and met. Let me say a bit about the passage of time.

The sense of the passage of time and the sense of aging are not identical, though as one goes through life they often are the warp and woof of experience. When you are waiting for someone who is late, the experience of time has a distinctive quality, but it is unrelated to the sense of aging. Usually we think of aging—the awareness that we are mortal, that there will be an end, and that we are pointed or running or being pulled toward it—as closely correlated with chronological age. We say that young children have little or no sense of aging, but this is not clinically or theoretically true.

A sense of aging develops early in life, although it is experienced fleetingly and takes quite a while to become an organizing and often agonizing magnet for experiences. When and how the sense of aging invades or merges into the sense of the passage of time, altering the perception of the future by shaping the present, is only partly an individual matter. Today, events in the larger society—for example, war, the spread of nuclear weapons, and pollution—have brought the two senses together for old and young alike.

I used to ask students this question, "I know how old you really are, but how old do you feel, or, for that matter, how young do you feel?" The answers fell into two categories. A typical example of the first is, "I feel older than I ever thought I would feel at this age, as if my best years are behind me, and from now on it won't be as good as it was in the past, which now looks better than I thought it did then." These answers were not meant to convey depressive feelings about the present or the future, but rather the belief that the future would be burdensome and its high points infrequent. The second and larger category would be typified by this answer, "I don't feel old, but I sure don't feel young. I look forward to getting into the real world, almost the way I felt about finishing high school and going away to college, but with this difference: inside me is that feeling that I may not get the breaks and I'll end up unhappy and bored and symbolically die well before my time." I have no basis for saying that *x* number of students are organizing their lives in terms of a young-old dichotomy. *But a sizeable number fear being trapped in life, and the word "trapped" conjures up imagery not only of confinement and impotence but of slow dying.*

When I was a student I didn't know about the "mid-career crisis" or what a personal disaster old age could be. I had old grandparents who were sick and dependent, but they were part of the family whose major aim was to love and protect them within the context of the family. I didn't think about old people as a group, much less as a "problem" group.

I would read the newspapers every day and listen to the radio (this was before TV), but they didn't tell me about nursing homes, gerontology, senior-citizen housing, Medicare, the "golden years," retirement as a legally sanctioned form of human abuse, and the loneliness of old people. Today this is standard fare in all the mass media—and depressing standard fare. Students not only know about the scandalous conditions of nursing homes; they see these homes on television.

About the only thing I can remember learning about old people was that they slowed down physically, that their memory for recent events was poor, and that they could be childish. Now the study of aging has become fashionable in the university, either as a field in itself or as a component of courses dealing with public and economic policy. In the past decade students have become acutely aware of aging in its social, familial, and personal aspects. Is it surprising that their heightened awareness has been infused with foreboding and cynicism? Is it unreasonable to assume that the sense of aging has already begun in these highly educated young people, and that their sense of the passage of time has become related to the sense that time is a limited resource already beginning to run out?

In all religions there is a ritual signifying the end of childhood and the beginning of adulthood. In days when religion was more central to living, the ceremony was a momentous event for the boy or girl, signifying arrival at a much-desired status and the opening of new sought-after responsibilities. Growing "up" referred not only to physical characteristics; "up" also meant the accumulation of knowledge and experience out of which would be shaped an enduring personal perspective leading to the good life. Today we see this no less clearly in our educational *system*: *Pre*-school or kindergarten, *first* grade, *second* grade, the years of *elementary* school, the *middle* school or *junior* high, *high* school, and then the different levels of *higher* education. What is significant is not only that the upward trajectory is not parabolic but that the process of growing "up" does not cease and begin to run "down." Indeed, every rationale advanced for prolonged education conveys the message that growth through formal education insures a similar experience of growth *after* formal education.

This rhetoric is no longer accepted by the young. The reasons are complicated, and not without an ironic twist. The fact is that students accept on a deep level the value of growth and of continuous growing up. But they see two obstacles: the nature and structure of education, and society's demand to conform to traditional values of success in the world of work. Far from not wanting to grow up, young people want to be assured that the opportunity for growth will be available through life. The past several decades could well be labeled "the Age of Personal Growth": the frenetic seeking for "growth experiences," "consciousness raising," "self-actualization," exploiting one's "human potential," and seeking "encounters" with oneself and others. The jargon multiplies, new techniques appear with dizzying rapidity, and the supermarket of "personal growth" products overwhelms the consumer who comes back again and again to sample the different brands. One could argue that far more than a need for growth is involved, and that, of course, is true. But the heavy emphasis by young people on the importance of growth, the fear of boredom, the terror of entrapment, and the anxiety over possible stagnation—these are variants of society's message that the more education one has, the more a person will have a right to experience life as a vibrant process of growing and not as a despairing descent to death. There is no message from society that one grows up as a preparation for running down. Nevertheless the process of continuing growth is by no means automatic. In fact, young people graduating from college today find an obstacle in their path that severely impedes their chances of growing. It is what I call "the one-life, one-career imperative"—the obligation of every person to decide from a smorgasbord of possibilities the *one* vocational dish that he or she will feed on for the rest of life. This has become so accepted a view in America, transmitted through parents and schools, that for most people it is a command—it must be obeyed. The dynamics are similar to those of marriage and divorce. It used to be that when one got married it was ordained—by religion and law—to be forever. If one did not believe that marriages were made in heaven, there was no doubt that they could not easily be undone on earth. One life, one partner. That has changed. *In fact, our culture has made it far easier to change marriage partners than to change careers.*

The necessity to make *one* career choice channels the power of personal growth into narrow confines, requiring individuals to construct plans and fantasies about how they can accommodate growth to the career chosen. These constructions often turn out to be an illusion, and the disillusionment brings in its wake a sense of regret, a dread that the doors of opportunity have already closed and that one must confront a future relatively devoid of vibrancy.

What I have been saying undergirds several conclusions. The first, and most obvious one, is that the women's liberation movement had the effect of steering many of them to careers other than in teaching, careers which they regarded as less confining, more likely to offer a more varied experience, more stimulating over the course of a lifetime, more exploitive of their talents and creativity. The second conclusion is that the same considerations were no less present in men. What was "in the air" of the sixties was absorbed by men. If there was no men's liberation movement, that should not obscure the fact that men, like women, rebelled against careers perceived to be narrow, stifling, and containing no ladder of personal growth. The third conclusion is that, as never before, young people had come to have an implicit, overarching goal in life, certainly in regard to career choice: They wanted to experience and learn more about themselves, others, and the "real world"; they wanted to feel that their career choice would always be challenging and satisfying.

Let us not forget that in the sixties the turmoil (a weak word!) on college campuses centered around many issues but the one most relevant here is that students wanted a voice in how educational policies and issues affecting them were resolved and made. That is to say, they were no longer content to be "just" students required to conform to what officialdom decided, to be viewed as too immature and inexperienced to have a say in their education. Students regarded officialdom in their colleges and universities precisely in the same way they regarded corporate America: disrespectful of individuality, impersonal, authoritarian or patriarchal or arbitrary, possessing a culture that was intellectually and personally confining, stultifying, and manipulative. It was during the sixties that a manuscript written by someone in California was akin to a best-seller on campuses. Its title was *The Student as Nigger.*

What I have said about colleges and universities also applies to secondary schools, although the rebellious turmoil there received less play in the mass media, which downplayed the expressed student opinion that high schools were boring, unstimulating places. And aware, as students all were, of what was happening on college campuses, they did not look with enthusiasm on going there. Indeed, beginning in the mid-sixties two changes were already manifest that were unheard of and heretofore disapproved. Many high school students wanted "time out" before going on to college, and college students also opted to take a year off during their college years, and many more wanted a hiatus between graduation and entering a graduate program. There was more than one motivating force for these changes, but certainly one of them was the desire to avoid what they saw as the perils of a lock-step educational system that sought to narrow their opportunities for personal growth, expression, and self-realization.

It is very important to note that, so far as I have been able to ascertain, *none* of the schools (or programs) in the performing arts were confronted with students clamoring for or demanding changes in their training or a voice in policy or decision making. I do not feel unjustified in suggesting that these students did not look at their present situation *or their future careers* with the foreboding characteristic of students generally.

Now let me answer the question with which this chapter began: What should be the overarching purpose of schooling, regardless of choice of future vocation, we wish the high school graduate to reflect or to have acquired? My answer is that I would want students to be motivated to learn more, to develop more, to experience personal and cognitive growth. Put in another way: They should possess the awe, wonder, and curiosity about themselves, others, and the world they had when they started school, characteristics they possessed but which went underground (or were extinguished) as they went from elementary to middle to high school.

I anticipate several criticisms of my overarching purpose. The first is that phrases like "to learn more, to develop more, to experience personal and cognitive growth" are laudable goals but how do you get at and "measure" them? In the history of psychological testing there are many examples about which such a criticism was initially expressed but over time significant headway was made, especially in the arenas of cognition, infancy and child development, personality, vocational aptitudes, attitudes, and more. The overarching goals above may be considered as attitudes. When I consider that psychologists have devised means for measuring damn near every human psychological characteristic, the above goals do not strike me as extraordinarily difficult to measure, bearing in mind that every test requires a process of correction and improvement. (It is the absence of that process which explains why the mountain of available tests contains so many that are totally or nearly worthless.) I find it strange indeed that means to measure the above goals have not been developed. In the course of a school year students are given many tests as measures of what they have learned. That, of course, is because for all practical purposes schools see their overarching purpose in terms of a very narrow conception of learning. How students feel about what they learn, the judgments they make about its significance, the place of those feelings and attitudes in their future perspective—are these factors of little importance in comprehending the import of achievement test scores? Do test scores in any way help us explain why over the course of school the level of boredom and motivation for school learning go downhill from the time when as kindergartners they wanted so much to learn what the world was about?

A second criticism of the overarching goal is that it is unrealistic and unfair because it assumes that factors external to schooling are or will be supportive of the goal; there are limits to what one should expect schools can accomplish without appropriate support from family, neighborhood, and community. Of course there are limits to *whatever* you consider as an overarching goal, but that does not explain, let alone justify, falling far short of it. My overarching goal is not utopian in that I expect all or most students to realize that goal. On the contrary, my argument is that the attitudes that goal reflects are held by an appallingly low number of students, thereby lessening the chances that any other educational goal will be approximated. It is no sin to fall short of the mark or goal, but it is a secular sin not to have an overarching goal you take very seriously. As I have said, schools have several goals but to act as if they are of equal importance or value is to subvert all of them.

The third criticism is less a criticism than a question: What does my overarching goal mean for teachers and teaching? I have discussed that question in previous books (Sarason, 1990b, 1993a, 1993b), and I shall not try to summarize them here. What I can indicate here are three features of a context for productive learning, features undergirding the overarching goal. The first is recognizing and respecting the individuality of the learner, i.e., where the learner is psychologically coming from and the attitudes, interests, and curiosities that implies. The second is that the teacher knows the subject matter well enough to know when or where the learner may have difficulty; the teacher is a preventer of problems, not a repairer. Third— and here is where the performing artistry of the teacher is so crucial—the teacher is always seeking ways to stimulate and reinforce the learner's wanting to learn and do more. I am in no way an advocate of mindless permissiveness and indulgence, and I recognize that the teacher has to be perceived by students as having standards and values he or she takes seriously. The artistry of teachers (and parents!) inheres in helping the student come to see those standards and values as his or her own, not something demanded, not something verbally expressed and to which there is a superficial, conforming response, but rather an assimilation into the learner's psychological bloodstream. Students know they are expected to learn. But is *knowing* in the absence of *wanting* the overarching goal of schooling? At the present time it is. The usual small number of exceptions aside, teachers rivet on knowing, not wanting, as in the case of Mr. Holland, but when a teacher takes wanting seriously, that teacher, again like Mr. Holland, becomes a performing artist whose goal is to captivate his or her audience, to get them to *want* to return, not to feel they *have* to return. Like any performing artist, the teacher wants to feel the audience has been satisfied, has been moved, has had a *personally* rewarding experience.

Another criticism takes the form of two questions. Where are you going to get these teachers who are and will always be in short supply? How will they be trained? The first question betrays a most unrealistic conception of institutional change as well as an equally unrealistic time perspective. The first step is to provide incentives and support for several programs willing to radically alter their selection criteria as well as their training methods. I say only several because they will be embarking on uncharted seas, the equivalent of the first telephone, the first airplane, the first computer, the first heart bypass or transplant. Initially the problem is not how to do it but to recognize that *we have to do it*, knowing that we will be starting with Model A, the bugs in which will require the development of Model B, and on and on in a self-correcting process. *That will take time and money*. The one feature these initial programs will share is a commitment to and agreement on the characteristics of a context of productive learning and its implications for selection and training. We cannot assume that there is one, and only one, tried and true approach. Nor can we assume that all trainees will end up equal in their artistry and effectiveness. But we can assume (and this is testable) that the *average* level of artistry and effectiveness of all trainees will be discernibly higher than trainees from conventional programs. And I also assume that if these programs are adequately supported—including fellowships for students—the pool of those you would seek to attract would not be small and, I predict, would grow. At the present time young people who are at or near the point of choosing a career do not perceive teacher preparatory programs in a positive light, i.e., it is easy to be admitted to one, the length of training (1–2 years) is not long, there are few challenges, it is a relatively easy way to get a job in schools where there are even fewer challenges, and teachers do not command the respect they were presumably accorded way back when. There has long been a debate about whether it should be mandatory that preparatory programs only admit college graduates, that undergraduate teaching programs do not leave sufficient time to obtain a firm grasp of subject matter, that 4 years of a liberal arts education are a necessary background for teaching. Without taking sides here in that debate, I have to say that the debate has totally ignored the significance of what I have called the overarching goal of schooling, an ignorance that does not allow either side of the debate to confront or explain why so many classrooms are boring disasters for students. I would say the same if the Ph.D. became a requirement in order to enter a preparatory program.

The final criticism again can be put in the form of a question: Even if your overarching goal is justified, what would students in these programs encounter in today's schools during and after their preparation? Have you not been a long and constant critic of what schools, generally speaking, do to teachers and students? I agree with the criticism, but does that mean we throw up our hands and give up any hope of improving our schools? The answer of course is no, which is why my last book was titled *Political Leadership and Educational Failure* (1998). That book makes four points:

1. The inadequacies of our schools are many, national, and a threat to the social fabric.
2. The reform efforts in the post World War II era have cost scores of billions (if not trillions) of dollars but with little consequence.
3. Over the decades no small number of people have become increasingly distrustful of and cynical about school improvement and educators. In recent years I have asked people this question: If you were starting from scratch, would you come up with school systems as they are? No one, but no one, has ever said yes, although none could say where he or she would start or would end up.
4. State and national political leaders have been well-intentioned in regard to and fiscally supportive of school change, but they are totally ignorant of the history of educational reform as well as the core problems of schools. In regard to other major societal problems, these leaders feel or are made to feel obliged to become knowledgeable about them. Education is the exception.

Unless and until political leaders begin to become knowledgeable about overarching goals and their relations to teaching, and unless and until they discharge the obligation of their offices to inform the citizenry about what needs to be *learned* and done, nothing of consequence will happen. From my perspective and values there is no leadership within the educational community, certainly not on a national level, and that has long been the case. In that book I give examples of what can happen when political leaders become aware of problems about which they had not been knowledgeable. (And by knowledgeable I do not mean scholarly.)

We expect presidents to be educators of the public and conveyers of a moral vision which obliges the public seriously to confront problems which threaten that vision. That is why a chapter in my book is titled "Thomas Jefferson: America's Only Serious Education President."

What does all this have to do with teaching as a performing art? Frankly, when I started this book I did not expect that I would have to take up issues central to my previous books. But the more I realized that my conception of teaching as a performing art would require criteria for selection and methods of training dramatically different than from conventional practice, I knew that what I was suggesting would encounter resistance, if not outright rejection, from various segments of the educational community. I have been guilty of not taking my previous writings seriously. No meaningful change in education has ever been greeted warmly; only those changes which are cosmetic or promise results which nourish the quick-fix mentality have been welcomed.

Leaving aside everything I have thus far said on this, can the reader identify a change in teacher preparatory programs that was other than requiring more courses, increasing the length of practice teaching, the use of competency tests for licensure? In the abstract I am not opposed to any of these. What I am opposed to is the assumption that any one of them, or all in combination, will produce teachers who can create and sustain contexts of productive learning, who know the difference between knowing and wanting, who understand why you start where children are and not with a predetermined, calendar-driven curriculum, who are ever vigilant about what the audience is thinking and feeling about what they are learning. Learning is a personal and interpersonal affair between teacher and students that lasts for at least a year. In a context of productive learning, that relationship is one in which the parties get to understand each other; the word *under* in *under*stand implies that each learns something about the other that goes behind or under appearances. In too many of our classrooms, especially in middle and high school, the body language of students is quite revealing of what they think and feel about learning.

I did not dream up out of whole cloth my conception of teaching as a performing art. It was forced on me after sitting in scores and scores of classrooms observing teachers, most of whom seemed to view their students as empty vessels that needed to be filled, directed, and controlled. It was a one-way street. Some were as extreme as Mr. Holland initially was, but in most cases the classroom was devoid of personal expression by students and teachers. Teachers taught the way they were taught, their performing style and repertoire were in a very narrow range. Students performed the way they thought the teacher expected them to behave: Appear interested and dutiful, work or appear to work hard, and ask no questions. I remind the reader of what I said in the previous chapter about videos of Japanese, German, and American classrooms. I stopped systematic observing in classrooms a decade ago. Those videos reminded me that you cannot go far wrong expecting that the more things change the more they remain the same.

In the July 1, 1998, *New York Times* there is a long article (Applebome, 1998) about Dr. James Comer, a psychiatrist who has devoted his life to child development and education. The scope, intensiveness, and comprehensiveness of his activist reform program require no comment from me. In that article he is quoted as saying:

> . . . my friends in education still begin by talking curriculum and instruction," he said. "All those things are important, but where's the kid? What's the kid like? What's going on with the kid? All of American education has left the development of the child out of it. We may pay it lip service, but for a whole number of reasons, the needs of the kid get ignored. . . .
>
> "My biggest problem with education is we see learning as a function of intelligence and will," he said. "If you have the intelligence and will, you will learn. If you don't, you won't. Well, it's not that simple.

I quite agree. It is obvious from what he says that what today passes for instruction—and the instruction in instruction—is woefully inadequate for taking seriously "Where is the kid? What is the kid like? What is going on with the kid?" Dr. Comer is not advocating that teachers take more child development courses, period. As an experienced child psychiatrist he knows well that such courses are, at best, starting points and that the crucial issue is how the would-be teacher can be helped to appropriately apply theory and research to real kids in a real classroom, both of which are embedded in a complicated community. As Dr. Comer knows from his years spent training child psychiatrists, as I know from my years of training clinical psychologists, application of knowledge is the opposite of a routine affair because it focuses on the many problems associated with going from book knowledge to action. Dr. Comer rightly says that believing that kids will learn if they have the intelligence and will is the grossest of simplifications. But as he and I know from training child psychiatrists and clinical psychologists, "intelligence and will" (all of which our trainees had in abundance) are very frail reeds on which to depend if the goal is to understand and help another person. I am not suggesting that teachers should become psychologists or psychiatrists, although they inevitably and unreflectively play those roles. Having said that, it in no way excuses the scandalously inadequate preparation of teachers in regard to the questions

Dr. Comer asks. We expect the performing artist to have acquired that degree of self-understanding in combination with a repertoire of skills that "moves" an audience and deepens their understanding of themselves, so that they feel they are part of the experience.

Artistry is not a thing or a formula. As a Supreme Court justice remarked, "I cannot define pornography but I know when I see it." That is why when I talk about teaching and contexts of productive learning I urge the reader to see *Mr. Holland's Opus*. And that is why in my book *Letters to a Serious Education President* (1993a) I urge him to support a year-long filming, day by day, of two classrooms: one taught by a teacher skilled as a performing artist and committed to the overarching goal I have discussed, and one taught by a conventional teacher. It is one thing to talk or write about teaching, it is quite another thing to observe it. What was so instructive about the videos I discussed in the previous chapter is that those who watched them were a diverse group, only one of whom had been a classroom teacher, and yet each of us was struck by the artistry of the Japanese teacher and the absence of artistry in the German and American teachers. The difference hit you in the face. It was as if words were not necessary.

CHAPTER 11

Students as Teachers

In an earlier book (Sarason, 1996a) I suggested that one of the ways of characterizing the post World War II era is as the Age of Redefinition of People as Resources. Whereas different groups of people had heretofore been seen as having no resources to contribute to societal functioning, or very few resources, or resources that could be only utilized within narrow, confined limits, these groups either redefined themselves or were redefined through the efforts of their partisan advocates. Women in general and nurses in particular, old people, racial and minority groups, social workers, handicapped individuals, and mentally retarded individuals are obvious examples that come to mind. Women in the military as pilots or in or near the battle scene, or in positions of corporate responsibility, or on the Supreme Court or in the national Congress, or as religious leaders of congregations, or as members or even leaders of a space mission, or prime ministers of nations? Before World War II most people considered such possibilities as the stuff of unbridled fantasy, more like nightmare than fantasy. Similarly, no one would have predicted that not long after the war ended, the nurses would no longer be content to be handmaidens to physicians and that they would declare their professional independence so that today there are nurses in private practice providing educational *and* psychotherapeutic services to the public; at the same time, hospital administration and policy witnessed a shift of power from physicians to nurses.

Very soon after the war a professional war started in the arena of mental health. Who should be "allowed" to provide psychotherapeutic services which by tradition (and even law) was the province of physicians? The long and short of it is that today clinical psychologists, clinical social workers, clinical nurses, marriage counselors, and school psychologists are major providers of a variety of mental health services. And in the past several years the American Psychological Association has advocated (successfully in some states) that specially trained clinical psychologists be permitted to write prescriptions for medication. As a very old clinical psychologist I have witnessed these and other professional wars, and I can assure the reader that a comprehensive explanation of these and other battles centering around redefinition is a complicated one. But one thing they all had in common was this stance: No longer will we be content to be defined as we have been in the past, we know and can do more than we have been permitted to do, we are redefining ourselves not for purposes of aggrandizement and desire for power but because we are capable of doing more than you think. The process of and pressure for redefinition—whatever its origins and wherever its advocates may be—can count on opposition because redefinition challenges long-standing traditions and institutional arrangements.

There is one exception when redefinition does not meet strong opposition and that is during war (like World War II) when the need for traditionally defined human resources cannot be met. What happened in the World War II years, both in and out of the military, is that many people found themselves in or were assigned to jobs for which they had little or no formal preparation or experience. This is not to say that people found or were placed in jobs blindly or cavalierly. (Although one seasoned veteran officer did say to me, "It was so bad during the early years of the war that if a recruit had one head, two eyes, and breathed, we had a place for him. Of course we made mistakes, but we were more surprised at how many of them learned to do what they never thought they could do, and they were just as surprised as we were. When you fight a war, you can't be fussy about credentials.")

The post World War II social changes had their origins, directly or indirectly, in the war years (Sarason, 1996a), and one of those changes was the process of redefinition of different groups as resources.

I started this chapter as I did as prologue to a proposal I shall make about students learning to teach: Students in middle and high schools will be encouraged to learn what is involved in teaching.[1] The idea of students as tutors and mentors of younger students has been taken seriously in some schools, but the purpose of this practice has not been to use it as an initial step in learning how to teach. That is to say, the purpose has been solely to help students at risk and not to further or broaden the intellectual and career education of the student tutors whose "rewards" are largely, if not exclusively, of a personal nature. Why has the use of students as tutors not spread? The reasons are many but one of them is how middle and high

---

1. As I will make clear later, my proposal is a complicated one because it not only requires programmatic and other changes in schools but in preparatory programs for teachers as well. The idea of students as teachers was suggested to me by Kenneth Wilson who, with Bennett Daviss, wrote the very seminal book *Redesigning Education* (1994).

school students are viewed as resources. Let me illustrate what I mean by several examples.

The first is a long-standing program in the Shoreham-Wading River middle school on Long Island in New York. A book about the program was written by a teacher, Mr. Vlahakis, *and* his students (Vlahakis et al., 1978).[2] In any one week approximately 300 of that middle school's 600 students spend several hours a week in a helping relationship in a community setting (such as nursing homes). Initially, the directors of these settings were very skeptical, to say the least, about students, on average 11–12 years of age, in an active relationship with old or handicapped individuals; these students could be a burden or a nuisance, perhaps even a danger, given their immaturity. But the arrangements were made in part because the teacher would act as supervisor as well as conduct sessions with the students, going over their responsibilities and duties as well as determining how the students were making personal and intellectual sense of their experiences. It did not take long before the directors said they would gladly take more students because they were providing a very valuable service. As the book indicates, there were memorable personal and educational experiences for the students who had never seen themselves as resources of use to others, just as others had viewed them as young, immature *children* whose place was in a classroom and school. Of course they were young, of course they were immature by adult standards, of course they would require close supervision, and of course there was no guarantee they would not make mistakes. But equally, of course, they were students with a burning curiosity about themselves in relation to an "outside" world which represented a challenge they wished to accept.

The second example (Butterworth & Weinstein, 1997) is a K–6 private, far-from-affluent school created by parents who ensured that there would be a significant number of minority students, many of whom would require tuition scholarships. In addition to the regular academic program (which differs perhaps by virtue of specialist teaching in the elementary grades and by the requirement of a second language), there existed a variety of additional programs which enhanced the daily classroom activities. These included student government, a school economy, publishing, theater performances, an outdoor education program, community experiences, an after-school program, and holiday celebrations.

The school had a system of student government in which a mayor, vice-mayor, secretary, treasurer, and social coordinator were elected by the whole

---

2. The book was generally not available and is out of print, which is why, with the permission of Mr. Vlahakis, I excerpted a large part of it for my book *You Are Thinking of Teaching?* (1993c).

school twice a year. Each individual running for office appointed a campaign manager who, along with the candidate, prepared a speech as well. Representatives from each class completed the membership of the governing body. Two teachers helped the students plan activities and fund-raisers for the school.

The school also had an economic system in which children held regular jobs around the school and were paid a weekly salary in the local scrip, "keybucks." Jobs ranged from aiding in the classroom or office to maintenance around the school grounds: adults in the school supervised jobs related to their interests and classroom/subject area needs. Jobs were listed, students wrote applications, and were interviewed for positions. Students could save keybucks in the bank (run by the sixth grade) or spend keybucks at the school store (run by the fifth grade) or bookstore (run by the fourth grade) and for field trips and the use of special equipment like computers.

Publishing was a third area of activity for the school. A student newspaper was published monthly, staffed by students from all the grades, and a literary magazine was published twice a year by the fourth grade. A yearbook with photographs was also published by a student staff with teacher help. The principal wrote a weekly Wednesday letter to parents and children, and classroom teachers routinely sent home newsletters about class activities.

During the year, two school-wide performances were held, a musical for the holiday season, and a dramatic or musical comedy at the end of the year. Scripts were modified so that every child in the school performed in the play. In addition, each grade put on a play for the school and for parents.

An outdoor education program involved fourth to sixth graders in a 5-day camping trip to an area of ecological importance and younger children in one-night camping trips. Class visits to community theatre, concerts, and museums were also regular parts of the program. Students brought their own performances to local homes for the aged. Community resources also visited the school, for example, two architects collaborated with fifth-grade students in designing a model community for their social studies assignment.

The year was also punctuated by celebration—Halloween parades, Thanksgiving luncheon, Martin Luther King's Birthday, Grandparent Day, and Graduation dinner, to list a few. These traditions have developed rich, elaborate rituals which brought energy to the school periodically during the year and warmly involved the family community.

The Butterworth and Weinstein description is of a setting in which what we could call "small kids" are given and accept duties and responsibilities rarely if ever given in public elementary schools. What the writers make clear is that the principal and teachers did not regard the students as *just* small kids unable to accept diverse responsibilities, too young and inexperienced to confront tasks that require initiative, planning, creativity, and cooperative endeavor. The students did not do what they did because it was required or demanded of them. Of course the teachers offered ideas, advice, and guidance, but that does not explain the enthusiasm, energy, and the accomplishments of the students. I had occasion to talk to two high school students who had attended that school, and they said that their years there were far more than what is ordinarily meant by "going to school." In fact, they said, their subsequent years in middle and high school were less challenging, required less initiative, and certainly provided less of that sense of community in which ideas and purposes could be tested in action. If I had to put it in my own words, what they seemed to be saying would go like this: "We were accorded that degree of respect that made it easy for us to engage in the variety of tasks and projects we did. We were not regarded as dependent, guidance seeking, dutiful kids from whom not much was expected. We were made to feel that we had something to contribute to each other and to the school."

The third example is about high school students. A colleague of mine, Dr. Richard Sussman, had obtained a master's degree in child development at Columbia's Teachers College. Several years later he visited a professor there whom he had found very helpful and stimulating. Dr. Sussman was interested in the current research program she and her graduate students were planning and doing. The professor described the research program which would require studies of elementary school children. She finished her account by saying that the research was not likely to be done because it would require a number of schools and most of those she had approached did not wish to cooperate. For purposes of brevity, here is what Dr. Sussman asked:[3]

1. If I can provide you with 10 or so selected high school students, would you explain to them the goals and significances of the research?
2. Would you train them to collect your data?
3. Would you give them a mini-seminar on data analysis?

The professor was predictably, understandably, more than surprised and skeptical. How could you trust high school students to collect research data? Was it not likely they would make errors of one kind or another? After all, the one thing we know is that they have had no experience in research

---

3. The rationale undergirding his questions would take us too far afield, but the interested reader will find that rationale in *Crossing Boundaries* (Sarason & Lorentz, 1998), a book to which Dr. Sussman contributed.

and the moral and scientific obligations of the researcher. After brief discussion Dr. Sussman played his trump card by saying, "If you can agree with what I have suggested, I can make available to you all the elementary schools you need." That research went so well that the students were invited to make a presentation at Teachers College and made a similar presentation to their board of education.

We pin labels on individuals and groups which implicitly define what they can do and what we can expect of them. And the implications of labels are either in the form of positive or negative self-fulfilling prophecies. In the positive form *you define and act* toward individuals (or groups) in ways that make it likely—we are dealing with probabilities—that they will be able to do what your label indicates they can do. In the negative form your definition says what this or that person *cannot* do, and you act in ways consistent with that label and definition, thus making it likely that you will "prove" the validity of the label or definition. (Chapter 7 about Schaefer-Simmern and artistic ability is an example of what can happen when a conventional definition of a group's capabilities is explicitly challenged.)

Inevitably we categorize, pigeon-hole, slot, and label people in terms of ability, aptitude, interests, motivation. That is certainly justified when we can point to credible efforts which have challenged the validity of our labels and support rather than undermine the labels we use. Unfortunately, however, we are frequently totally unaware that we apply our labels on the basis of custom, or our socialization into our culture, or conventional wisdom which is certainly conventional but not necessarily wise, or sheer prejudice. I did not present the three examples to convey the impression that labeling and defining (and their implications) are inherently pernicious or unwarranted. My purpose rather was a form of plea, specifically in regard to students in our schools, that we re-examine the ways we define them as resources because if we do so we are very likely not only to begin to redefine them, but to understand more clearly the obstacles that institutional custom and practice place in the ways of taking the redefinition process seriously. So let me after this long prologue present my proposal for students as beginning teachers.

My proposal calls for an eight-year study in which, beginning in the third year of the study, 10 students are chosen by criteria indicating that they might be capable of performing a teaching function in the classroom, which in no way means that they would be teaching their peers but rather students in lower grades. Nor does it mean that by the end of the initial study they would have demonstrated other than a very circumscribed but real teaching function. And by *real* I mean that if you sat in the classroom, you would not be in doubt that they are endeavoring to teach something of educational value.

I said that selection would begin in the third year of the study for several reasons. The most obvious reason, of course, is that those who will be participants in developing a course of action will have had no previous experience to use as a guide. They will confront many knotty questions. What grade should we start with? Should we initially start the students in one-on-one relationships, and if so, how would we want to differentiate that experience from what we call tutoring? If, as we hope, they will learn to perform in a classroom, what do we have to do to help them gain an understanding of what has been learned about learning? And to gain that understanding how do we help them to use their own educational experiences? The aim is not to give them a course in the psychology of learning but rather in a step-by-step fashion over several years to make them sensitive to the fact that what a teacher does or does not do is a direct reflection of how a teacher thinks, and in addition, that for any aspect of subject matter the teacher has to know that aspect very, very well. How and when do you begin this learning about learning process? How and when do you start to help them see and accept the fact that teaching is an art, a performing one, requiring of the teacher imagination and a grasp of where the learner is coming from, a grasp the sources of which are both cognitive and intuitive? Because the student is, after all, a student who is learning other subject matter, what would be the minimal time the student should devote as a study participant, a minimum below which subverts the goals of the study? Besides *Mr. Holland's Opus*, what other visual aids would be intrinsically interesting and instructive as a basis for discussing teaching and learning? Should we, as I think we should, in each succeeding year of the study select 10 new participants because of our obligation to learn from the mistakes and inadequacies exposed by experience with previous cohorts?

Those are but a sample of the questions that would confront such a study. I assume other questions have occurred to the reader who, I would suggest, should start with what I consider the most important question: Are the goals of this study so far out in left field, so unrealistic about the ability (and perhaps even the motivation) of these students, so utterly impractical that if you had to vote on whether to fund, not a study, but a planning grant to examine the issues involved, you would cast a negative vote? If so, that would mean, to me at least, that you are unable or unwilling to consider redefining students as possessing resources of potentially significant value to the school and its students. Furthermore, it would confirm what I said in a previous book (1993c) in a chapter titled "The Non-Reading Professional": Teachers read very little of the education literature; they are, generally speaking, unaware of research reports and other types of accounts which clearly suggest that we underestimate what students can do and want to do. Those reports do not constitute a basis for saying that my pro-

posal should be warmly embraced, but they do constitute a basis for saying that my proposal is neither unrealistic nor outlandish. That the proposal challenges conventional views of the ability of students and their role
in a classroom and school is obvious, but it is not a challenge that deserves
out of hand rejection as pie-in-the-sky musings. Let us not forget that one
way you can write human history is as a series of battles centering around
the question: What are people capable of learning and doing? So, for example, take the question of whether people—all people, not only ruling
elites—should have a voice in governance. Up until the eighteenth century
the answer was a clear no; you could not trust people to make wise decisions about governance; they were too inexperienced in the ways of the
world, they were too gullible and too ignorant to be given responsibility.
Besides, they not only needed to be ruled with a firm hand, they wanted
such rule, they wanted to be told what to think and do. Even today, there
are many places on this earth where that battle continues. I am not contending that all challenges to how we define individuals and groups are of
equal merit. I am contending that my proposal does have that degree of
merit as to be taken seriously in action. The purpose of this chapter is to
provide an underlying rationale for my proposal, not to take up the methods and research design of an initial study. There is no one best way to
proceed in a study for which previous experience gives us no guide as to
method and evaluation and more. When I say that this has to be viewed as
an exploratory study, "exploratory" does not excuse sloppiness, diffuse-
ness, or an undue dependence on opinion or anecdote. And precisely because of the importance of such a study, it should not be undertaken unless
there are sufficient time and funding to do justice to it. We have had a surfeit of initial studies in education where the pressures of time and money
contributed to compromises that made it virtually impossible to come to
any secure conclusion about the findings. An initial study is not a fishing
expedition, it is a reasoned exploration which should determine when, if,
and how further studies should be conducted.

My proposal raises some very practical issues of which the most important is: Who will have responsibility for working with and overseeing
the students? Before you can think about that question there has to be agreement on three points: Teachers do not have time to be other than part time
participants; not every teacher has the motivation, knowledge, and interpersonal skills to instruct, guide, mentor these students; the goal of the
study is *not* to select and train tutors but to provide these students with a
degree of understanding about learning and teaching which will allow
them, albeit in a *circumscribed* way and time, to teach a class of younger
students. I italicized circumscribed to emphasize the obvious point that we
would not be training teachers but young people for the purpose of pro-

viding them the opportunity to begin to experience and comprehend what teaching requires.

Over the decades I have gone to see student productions of plays and musicals. In each instance the students were selected by a teacher-director who, I assume, was not compensated (or was very minimally compensated) for this extracurricular activity. That teacher-director was essentially self-selected, it was something they wanted to do. Although the audience was never in doubt that they were witnessing an amateur performance, several things were noteworthy. First, the students were giving their all; to say they were luxuriating in the opportunity to perform is no exaggeration.[4] Second, some of those productions were surprisingly good, leading me and others to say (proudly), "Some of those kids have what it takes to become real actors." Third, in a few of these atypical instances I knew the teacher-director, and therefore, I was not surprised by what they got out of their cast. They went far beyond ensuring that their students knew their lines; they would make an effort to explain the "psychology" of the role and the importance of timing, facial expression, body language, and voice projection; they encouraged students to imagine the kinds of feelings of the person they were portraying. (Some of these teacher-directors were members of a community amateur theatrical group.) All of this is by way of saying that I have known teachers who I believe had what it takes to do justice to the students in my proposal. The degree to which that kind of teacher could participate in the study would depend on funding. In an initial study of much potential significance, the first question should be: *What do we need to know, have, and do in order to be able to determine at the end of the study that we are on the right road, that we should be allowed to learn and do, or that further expenditure of funds is not justified?* Ignoring that caveat is precisely why I wrote *Charter Schools: Another Flawed Educational Reform?* (1998) because proponents of charter schools had (and have) a grievously unrealistic conception of the inadequacies of the resources charter school legislation imposed. I hope I am wrong in my predictions that (1) the majority of charter schools will fall far short of their mark, and (2) we will never know why one charter school was successful and another was not. In the case of charter schools, I should hasten to add, unrealistic funding was but one reason for my predictions.

Who should have responsibility for developing and implementing such an initial study? There are more than a few *individuals* in our colleges

---

4. In Chapter 4 I noted that it is by no means unusual for professional actors to say that their choice of career had its seeds in their middle and high school experiences in student production. This, as I shall discuss later, is one of the consequences I would hope would be true for some of the students in regard to choice of teaching as a career.

and universities who would be appropriate because they know schools and their culture, they truly understand young students; they are careful observers, investigators, and reporters; they have worked with or have participated in the preparation of teachers (or both); they are imaginative people with interpersonal, diplomatic skills; they are serious workers whose ideas and investigative programs attract others to them either as students or colleagues; they are risk takers. Some are in schools of education, some in departments of psychology, some in institutes of child development. I would have no trouble coming up with a list of *individuals* who, if they were interested, would do justice to the study. They have a proven track record, they are well known to others in their arena of interests and work. It would be a list of individuals and not of places or institutions because it would be an egregious indulgence of parochialism to think that because it is a study of students and schools the responsibility for it should be given to a school of education. Only a few of the individuals on my list are in such schools. I could come up with a short list of school teachers I have known who could play a very important role in such a study but who lack the knowledge and experience to be given the responsibility of an action research program. The list is short for the obvious reason that although I have had occasion to observe and know many scores of teachers, they are a very minute sample of the approximately 2 million people who teach in our schools.

I have talked about a single study but only to simplify this discussion. There should be several such studies and for two reasons. First, precisely because we cannot count on previous experience and an extant literature, and because each of the several sites predictably will proceed in different small and large ways—there is no one best way to proceed—we will learn more than if there is only one site. Second, it should be made possible for each site to be in meaningful contact with the others: to be able to observe and learn from each other; not only on the level of ideas and method but also on the level of personnel exchange as well. Differences in approach are virtues to be protected, but that does not rule out cooperation. You learn a lot when you design an appliance, a car, or a program, and one of the things you learn, and it is the most important thing, is how to capitalize on what you have learned for the purpose of *redesign*. That is why Kenneth Wilson titled his seminal book *Redesigning Education* (1994).

Some readers may have asked themselves why my proposal is about students in middle and high schools where it is not unusual for students to serve as tutors and even perform a community service. Although I would have no objection to starting in high school, I prefer starting in middle school because it is in those years that so many students begin to lose interest in and motivation for school learning because (among other things) so much of what they learn has no particular personal relevance; it is for so many of them arid book knowledge which tells them little about themselves or others or what to them is the unexplored world. They are told they are no longer "children" in elementary school but not big or mature like high school students, a message that implies they cannot be given meaningful responsibility for almost anything except to learn what they are told to learn. It is, in my opinion, an example of a negative self-fulfilling prophecy. I am again reminded here of the enthusiasm, seriousness, and energy middle school students manifest when they engage in dramatic productions, especially in those instances where the students had a voice in choosing the play or musical to be performed, or in instances similar to those I described earlier. If my proposal should turn out to achieve even modest, positive results, it should dispel any doubts that similar efforts with high school students will be even more productive. I prefer to start with students with whom "conventional wisdom" says the outcomes will be uniformly negative, which is by way of saying that I like to operate on the basis of the dynamics of the positive self-fulfilling prophecy. But I must say again that I have no principled objections to starting with high school students. The important point and task is to start.

Imagine for the moment (if you can!) that the studies, at whatever levels from which students are chosen, produce credible, positive results. That is to say, the students gain an increased understanding of themselves in relation to the nature and complexity of learning and teaching; they know they are not teachers and they also know that far more is involved in teaching than knowing subject matter, that between teacher and pupil is a demanding process requiring the teacher to be a performer ever sensitive and adaptable to what his or her audience is thinking and feeling. If they have manifested increased understanding and a very modest level of competence, they have also acquired both humility and respect for the nature of learning and teaching.

So what? Assuming that these studies begin to have a *general* impact—that these studies do not, as most studies usually do, remain a local affair—then teachers of "younger" pupils have a pool of "older" pupils who can be helpful to them. Teachers have fallen into three groups when I presented my proposal to them. One group almost instantly and unequivocally agreed that using the older students would be a pain in the neck, their contributions not compensated by the time and responsibility the teacher would have to assume. Not a few of these teachers regarded the proposal as outlandish. The second group consisted of teachers who were intrigued but balked at the idea that these students should ever be permitted to teach a class, however circumscribed in time and scope it may be. They had no trouble with using them as one-on-one tutors—indeed they would welcome them as tutors—but not ever as "teachers." As almost all of them said, "I have pupils who are at risk to whom I cannot give the attention they need, so if I had tutors with some training, it would be a boon. But to help and supervise students teach a class is asking too much of the teacher and student." The third group, smaller than either of the first two, in one or another way said, "That would be an interesting challenge that would introduce novelty into my days, especially if a few other teachers in my school went along and we formed a working group. But I would not participate unless I knew my principal, other higher-ups, and parents were solidly supportive." This third group consisted of no more than 20% of the teachers, a fact that I found both surprising and encouraging. I should add that one teacher in this group said that she had given up on preparatory programs for teachers and that school systems should select and train their own teachers "so why not start with students in the system?"

My proposal challenges our accustomed way of defining the interests, aptitudes, and abilities of students. I am reminded here of many middle and high school teachers—and a few elementary teachers—who are astounded and chagrined that they have students who can use computers better and more creatively than they can; indeed in some instances the student has taught the teacher. The reaction of teachers stems in part from *their* view of how complicated learning to use the computer can be, and in part from the way they regard the capacities of their young students. Teachers are not alone in this respect. Most teachers are women and are familiar with the past history of how women were narrowly defined in terms of work and career. But they, like most of us, may know a lesson from history but do not generalize it to other groups. More to the point of this chapter are those studies which have demonstrated that carefully selected individuals can effectively conduct brief psychotherapy (with circumscribed goals) even though they have had no formal training. More important than the labels appended to the kind of work in which they were normally engaged, were the kinds of people they were: sensitive, supportive, nonconfrontational, capable of listening and engendering trust.

My proposal, if the results are positive and accepted and implemented generally, can increase the number of people who seek a career in education for the best of reasons: they have had experiences that indicated a match between their interests and aptitudes and teaching young people. As I pointed out in previous chapters, in the conventional performing arts the individual's interests in a career in this or that performing art begin early in life. That is infrequently the case among those who choose teaching as a career, which in part (and only in part) explains why many teachers come to wish they had chosen another career path.

As I was writing this chapter I saw on July 12, 1998, a one hour program on C-SPAN in which Dr. Peter Gomes, minister of Harvard's Memorial Church, discussed his most recent book *Biblical Wisdom for Everyday Living* (1998). It was one of the most interesting programs I have ever seen, if only because in that one hour he illustrated most of the points I have made in this book. Here are some of the points he makes directly or indirectly in his book:

1. Preaching is a performing art.
2. Most preaching is a routinized affair to which the audience gives dutiful attention but finds uninteresting, personally irrelevant, and not thought-provoking. Too often the preacher has similar feelings.
3. The preacher has a "curriculum," the Bible which, of course, he or she should have mastered, but a mastery that reflects a process of personal assimilation and significance which serves as a basis for thinking and planning about how to make the curriculum alive for the audience. Telling the audience what is in the Bible is one thing, the easy part, but unless the preacher can make the text timely and of concrete significance to the audience—and that may or should include the preacher's personal experiences in comprehending the text—no bond is formed between preacher and audience. Dr. Gomes takes a dim view of histrionics because however such histrionics may be interesting, it diverts attention away from grappling with the task, which is what it is all about.
4. Preachers have to be knowledgeable about and even sensitive to the audience and its reactions, just as actors have to be. Audiences are not homogeneous in regard to why they come to church. The more a preacher knows about the sources of heterogeneity, the more he or she should be obliged creatively to speak to those sources.
5. Learning to be a preacher is a developmental process: personally, intellectually, and theologically. And that is also the goal the preacher should have for his or her audience. The preacher is a teacher who, if he or she truly understands the audience, will be taught by them.

Dr. Gomes is a teacher in Harvard's divinity school. He described a seminar he conducts which is restricted to eight students, half of whom are beginning students and half advanced ones. It is obvious from his description that he takes the development of his students' qualities as performers as seriously as he takes subject matter, which is to say that he takes both very seriously.

I am aware that in this chapter I have given reasons why my proposal should be given a serious hearing because of its implications for teaching in schools. The proposal, however, goes far beyond teaching and schools because it speaks to a millennia-old issue: What are people capable of learning and doing? How must we learn to challenge our accustomed labels which tell us what people cannot learn and do? Why have we learned so little from the history of slavery, women, personal liberty, and democratic institutions? At the end of the nineteenth century an eminent physicist said that all of the important physical laws had been discovered. Famous last words.

CHAPTER 12

Criticism and Scapegoating

There is a difference between criticism and scapegoating. Scapegoating is the unjustified assignment of blame to an individual or group, thus ignoring, often deliberately, the contribution of others. When that assignment of blame is not deliberate, the scapegoating reflects a gross ignorance or oversimplification of a very complicated state of affairs. Criticism can shade into scapegoating, but we expect that someone labeled as "critic" has a basis in knowledge and experience which prevents that critic from scapegoating. We may not agree with the critic, but we do not want to conclude that he or she has done a "hatchet job," or conducted a vendetta, or has contributed nothing to our understanding of the issues. Critics are entitled to their opinions, but they are not entitled to forget the differences between criticism and scapegoating.

In this book I have studiously avoided scapegoating teachers, schools, school systems, and preparatory programs. There are no villains; no group has "willed" the current state of educational affairs. Anyone who has read my previous books will know that I believe the villain is an educational *system* comprised of teachers and administrators; boards of education; colleges and universities; state departments of education; national, state, and local legislators and executives; and, of course, parents. If an effective system means a coordinated, non-adversarial, self-correcting arrangement of parts, then the current system has to be given a failing grade. It is the villain in the sense that no significant change in any of its parts is possible unless that change takes into account and deals with the stultifying features of the current system. That is why my recent book *Political Leadership and Educational Failure* (1998) is based on my belief that nothing positive can occur unless the highest echelons of our political system make it their obligation to become more knowledgeable about what we call our educational system. By *knowledgeable* I do not mean sophisticated or scholarly but rather a level of understanding which will allow them to exercise moral leadership to alert the citizenry to several things: The post World War II reform movement has had minimal consequences, we can no longer afford to tinker at the edges, the present system is not self-correcting but rather inimical to change, and we have to be prepared to move in new and bold ways. That kind of leadership has been absent.

I wrote this book for two reasons, one theoretical and one practical, the latter deriving from the former. The theoretical reason is that the fruits, positive or negative, of any non-cosmetic change will be determined by the quality of teaching. In a literal ultimate sense, any intended change should be reflected in changes in how well teachers understand and are prepared to act consistent with that intended change. You can change curricula, reduce class size, resort to block programming, and more, but unless teachers are better prepared to create and sustain contexts of productive learning, the intended changes will not occur. That is why I regard what I have written in this book as practical, because it speaks to issues of selection and preparation which have received little or no attention even though teachers are never in doubt that they are performers with an audience. But what do we or they mean by performing? What conceptual rationale should inform the selection and preparation of teachers as performing artists? How do we capitalize on what has been learned about "performing" in the conventional performing arts? If I have not provided comprehensive answers to any of these questions, it does not mean they are impractical questions. The beginning steps to answers can begin tomorrow, knowing today that arriving at answers will take place over years.

For the sake of illustration let us assume that global warming is a valid phenomenon, which is to say that we have to admit that we and others in the "global village" have played a role. *Mea culpas* will not get us far. If global warming becomes a valid fact, it will not be because this or that country deliberately set out to produce the phenomenon, although there have been those who warned us that we could not continue as we were accustomed to. But if global warming becomes a fact and not an assumption, there are steps we *know* we will have to take even though those steps will be difficult, will require changes in how we "do business," and will take time. But we would not be without ideas of where we should begin.

I am certainly not the first person to assert that of all the major obstacles to educational reform, the selection and preparation of teachers are the most crucial ones, the ones the educational system has been unable or unwilling to confront. If they are the crucial issues, they do not, of course, possess for people the immediacy or compellingness that global warming would if it should be demonstrated as more than an assumption. There are people who view educational reform as a lost cause and look very favorably on vouchers, charter schools, and other "answers." And there are some people who would not be distressed at the demise of the public schools. Someone once said that it is hard to be completely wrong and that is how I view these advocates. Any proposal which assumes that you do not have to confront and deal with changes in the selection and preparation of teachers is doomed to be generally ineffective over the short and long term.

Scapegoating of teachers and schools has a long history. For example, after World War II we were witness to damning criticism of the public schools and teachers which reached a crescendo when the Soviet Union put the first orbiting capsule into space. New curricula were demanded and developed, a former president of Harvard wrote articles and books on what a comprehensive high school should be, and teacher preparatory programs were pressured to increase and emphasize courses in subject matter and de-emphasize what were called "Mickey Mouse" courses in methods. There was something akin to a Great Debate. On the one side were critics, mostly from universities, who were not always able to hide their demeaning assessment of teachers. On the other side were mostly educators who agreed that efforts at change were justified but whose proposals were (in my opinion) cosmetic. No one on either side had basically anything new or constructive to say about the adequacy of teacher preparatory programs except, of course, to assert that a more solid grasp of subject matter (taking more courses) would improve the quality of teaching. In some unexplained way the knowledge of teachers would stimulate the hearts and minds of students. There was absolutely no recognition that *maybe* teaching required more than a solid grasp of subject matter, that *maybe* the teacher as performer needed to be analyzed and judged in regard to the selection and preparation of teachers. In brief, teaching was a relatively simple affair devoid of artistry. I am sure that, if pressed, those who conveyed this view would have said, as William James said loud and clear more than a hundred years ago, that teaching was an art. But then as today the words *art* and *artistic* refer to a mysterious creative process that defies analysis and understanding, *thus dealing with process by ignoring it.*

Yes, I am quite aware that my stance in this book has been a very critical one which will not be greeted warmly in some quarters. And, yes, I do not believe that I have treated the issues exhaustively. My sole aim has been to persuade the reader that a long-neglected problem, a truly basic problem, should no longer be ignored or treated lightly, that on the levels of conceptualization and action (theory and practice) it is a thorny, frustrating, fascinating problem that will be better clarified by others if and when the problem is seen as a problem. Of one thing I am certain: If the problem stays in limbo, the scapegoating of teachers will mightily escalate, a sad example of blaming the victim.

I regard what I have said in this book as glimpses of the obvious, but it took me years to truly take the obvious seriously. I began my professional career as a psychologist in a spanking new, state institution for mentally retarded individuals. What quickly became obvious to me was that the employees who were in the closest and most sustained relationships with the residents were the attendants whose formal "care-taking" credentials were zero. A small number of them were well-meaning parent surrogates but most of them had little education, a poor work history, and little or no understanding of the residents for whom they were responsible. They were hired because they were available and would work for little pay, which is why the labor turnover in all state residential institutions was astronomical. The deinstitutional movement after World War II was a direct response to the recognition that these institutions were warehouses of human misery which were intractable to change. I knew about these institutional warehouses before I took my first position; I had interned in one of them (a state mental hospital) and had visited many more. I took that position precisely because the institution was new and was based on a rationale explicitly designed to avoid warehousing. When after 4 years I left to go to Yale, the institution was on the road to becoming a warehouse. Within 2 decades the situation was such as to require action and supervision of the courts.

What I failed to appreciate at the time was the obvious point that no one (which includes me) identified as a central and major problem that those who spent the most time with the residents had received no help, direction, or training. It never even came up in discussion that those on the bottom of the power hierarchy needed and deserved the opportunity to develop and enlarge their capabilities.

Teachers are not attendants. They are educated and possess formal credentials. They regard themselves as professionals, which is to say they have something to "profess" in regard to children and schooling. Their reward is not money but a sense of competence and accomplishment. Unlike attendants, they enter their profession with expectations of personal, intellectual, professional growth, as well as of respect and recognition for what they do. And, crucially, they expect to be part of a community of teachers whose interrelationships will be a source of stimulating growth. Several questions arise:

1. Why do so many teachers quickly conclude that few of those higher up in the power hierarchy have any interest in what they do, especially in our urban schools?

2. Why do teachers generally regard staff development days or workshops as token gestures long on irrelevance and boredom and short on practical help?
3. Why do teachers quickly learn that the culture of schools is inimical to any sense of professional collegiality?
4. Why do so many teachers begin to "burn out" after several years of teaching, and why do so many eagerly look forward to retirement? And why after 2 or 3 years do so many teachers leave the field?
5. Why do teachers generally come to regard preparatory programs in very negative terms? And why do they similarly regard the courses they take for continuing education credits?

None of these questions have a simple answer. But all of these questions imply or directly point to the interaction between the complexity I call the school culture and the many inadequacies of preparatory programs. Over the years I have written about that interaction and I have had many opportunities to present my views to audiences of educators. Although I may have heard what I wanted to hear, it has been my distinct impression that my views were favorably received. But it is also my distinct impression that on the level of policy and action my views have had little or no impact. If that disappoints me, it certainly does not surprise me. I do not expect this book to have a different fate. Indeed, this book increases the complexity of the issues because conceptualizing teaching as a performing art clearly means that preparatory programs will have to undergo a radical transformation. We are used to hearing that school change should only be attempted by those with a bottomless need for masochistic pleasures, a variant of the quip that no good deed goes unpunished. If school change is far more than a daunting task, the same can be said for changing colleges and universities in which preparatory programs exist. I have always found it ironically amusing that in the post World War II era school change has been high on the social agenda, with the consequence that the public rivets on schools as if our colleges and universities are not part of the problem. And matters are not helped any by the tendency of members of colleges and universities grossly to oversimplify what is at issue and at stake. Earlier in this era they oversimplified the problem by assuming that it could be "solved" by money. And throughout this era there have been those who proclaimed that if teachers had a more solid grasp of subject matter, the clouds would part and the sun would shine. Both oversimplifications were articulated by well-meaning people, but there is nothing in the record that disconfirms Mencken's caveat that for every important social problem there is a simple answer that is wrong.

I have always regarded blaming teachers as a clear example of blaming the victim. This book was written for several reasons, and chief among them was the opportunity once again to explain why I regard teachers as victims and, therefore, why so many of their students also become victims. There are no villains. If there were, the problems would not be as intractable as they are.

References

Alpert, H. (1990). *The life and times of Porgy and Bess: The story of an American classic.* New York: Knopf.

Applebome, P. (1998, July 1). Pleading a case for the child. *New York Times.*

Barker, R. G., & Gump, P. V. (1964). *Big school, small school.* Stanford: Stanford University Press.

Blumenthal, R. (1998, March 21). So you want to be a star? *New York Times.*

Butterworth, B., & Weinstein, R. (1997). Enhancing motivation and opportunity in elementary school. *Elementary School Journal, 97,* 57–80.

Dewey, J. (1934). *Art as experience.* New York: Menton and Balch.

Dreifus, C. (1998, July 14). Science is serious business to the "Mel Brooks" of physics. *New York Times.*

Fried, R. (1995). *The passionate teacher: A practical guide.* Boston: Beacon Press.

Garner, W. R., Hunt, H. F., & Taylor, D. W. (1959). Education for research in psychology. *American Psychologist, 14,* 167–179.

Garrison, J. (1997). *Dewey and eros: Wisdom and desire in the art of teaching.* New York: Teachers College Press.

Gilbert, S. (1997, December 23). Forget about bedside manners. Some doctors have no manners. *New York Times.*

Gomes, P. (1998). *Biblical wisdom for everyday living.* New York: William Morrow.

Greene, M. (1978). *Landscapes of learning.* New York: Teachers College Press.

Greene, M. (1988). *The dialectic of freedom.* New York: Teachers College Press.

Greene, M. (1995). *Releasing the imagination: Essays on education, the arts, and social change.* San Francisco: Jossey-Bass.

Gurewitsch, M. (1997, October). Maria, not Callas. *Atlantic Monthly,* pp. 103–107.

Heckman, P. (1996). *The courage to change: Stories from successful school reform.* Newberry Park, CA: Corwin Press.

Heyward, D. (1925). *Porgy.* New York: George H. Doran.

Huggett, R. (1969). *The truth about 'Pygmalion'.* New York: Random House.

James, W. (1902). *Talks to teachers on psychology: And to students on some of life's ideals.* New York: Henry Holt.

Jersild, A. (1955). *When teachers face themselves.* New York: Teachers College Press.

Koch, K. (1970). *Wishes, lies, and dreams: Teaching children to write poetry.* New York: Chelsea House.

Koch, K. (1977). *I never told anybody: Teaching poetry writng in a nursing home*. New York: Random House.

Little, S. W., & Cantor, A. (1970). *The playmakers*. New York: Norton.

Montera, V. (1996). Bridging the gap: A case study of the home-school-community relationship at the Ochoa Elementary School. Unpublished doctoral dissertation, College of Education, University of Arizona, Tucson.

National Commission on Teaching and America's Future (1996). *What matters most: Teaching for America's future*. New York: Author.

Nemy, E. (1985, April 15). O'Neill performed for Mayo doctors. *New York Times*.

Pauly, E. (1991). *The classroom crucible: What really works, what doesn't, and why*. New York: Basic Books.

Raimy, V. (Ed.) (1950). *Training in clinical psychology*. Englewood Cliffs, NJ: Prentice-Hall.

Rogers, C. (1942). *Counseling and psychotherapy: Newer concepts in practice*. Boston: Houghton-Mifflin.

Sarason, S. B. (1948). *Psychological problems in mental deficiency*. New York: Harpers.

Sarason, S. B. (1977). *Work, aging, and social change*. New York: Free Press.

Sarason, S. B. (1985). *Caring and compassion in clinical practice*. Northvale, NJ: Jason Aronson.

Sarason, S. B. (1989). *The making of an American psychologist*. San Francisco: Jossey-Bass.

Sarason, S. B. (1990a). *The challenge of art to psychology*. New Haven, CT: Yale University Press.

Sarason, S. B. (1990b). *The predictable failure of educational reform*. San Francisco: Jossey-Bass.

Sarason, S. B. (1993a). *Letters to a serious education President*. Newberry Park, CA: Corwin Press.

Sarason, S. B. (1993b). *The case for change: Rethinking the preparation of educators*. San Francisco: Jossey-Bass.

Sarason, S. B. (1993c). *You are thinking of teaching?* San Francisco: Jossey-Bass.

Sarason, S. B. (1994). *Psychoanalysis, General Custer, and the verdicts of history*. San Francisco: Jossey-Bass.

Sarason, S. B. (1995). *Parental involvement and the political principle*. San Francisco: Jossey- Bass.

Sarason, S. B. (1996a). *Barometers of change*. San Francisco: Jossey-Bass.

Sarason, S. B. (1996b). *Revisiting "The culture of the school and the problem of change."* New York: Teachers College Press.

Sarason, S. B. (1998). *Charter schools: Another flawed educational reform?* New York: Teachers College Press.

Sarason, S. B. (1998). *Political leadership and educational failure*. San Francisco: Jossey-Bass.

Sarason, S. B., Davidson, K., & Blatt, B. (1987). *The preparation of teachers: An unstudied problem in education* (enlarged ed.). Cambridge, MA: Brookline Books. (Original work published 1962)

Sarason, S. B., Levine, M., Goldenberg, J., Cherlin, D., & Bennett, E. (1966). *Psychology in community settings*. New York: John Wiley.

Sarason, S. B., & Lorentz, E. (1998). *Crossing boundaries*. San Francisco: Jossey-Bass.

Sato, M. (1992). Japan. In H. B. Leavitt (Ed.), *Issues and problems in teacher education: An international handbook* (pp. 155–168). Westport, CT: Greenwood Press.

Schaefer-Simmern, H. (1961). *The unfolding of artistic activity.* Berkeley, CA: University of California Press. (Original work published 1948)

Stanislavski, C. (1936). *An actor prepares.* New York: Theater Arts Books.

Susskind, E. C. (1970). *Questioning and curiosity in the elementary classroom* (Doctoral dissertation, Yale University, 1969). Ann Arbor, MI: University Microfilms International.

Thomas, G. (1997). What's the use of theory? *Harvard Education Review, 67*(1), 75–104.

Vaidya, L. (1998). *Alone on the stage: Reflections, writing, and the art of teaching.* Unpublished paper.

Vlahakis, R., et al. (1978). *Kids who care.* Oakdale, NY: Dowling College Press.

Waller, W. (1932). *The sociology of teaching.* New York: John Wiley.

Wilson, K. & Daviss, B. (1994). *Redesigning education.* New York: Henry Holt.

About the Author

Seymour B. Sarason is professor of psychology emeritus in the Department of Psychology and at the Institution for Social and Policy Studies of Yale University. In 1962 he founded and directed the Yale Psycho-Educational Clinic, one of the first research and training sites in community psychology. Fields in which he has made special contributions include mental retardation, culture and personality, projective techniques, teacher training, anxiety in children, and school reform. His numerous books and articles reflect his broad interests.

Dr. Sarason received his Ph.D. degree from Clark University in 1942 and holds honorary doctorates from Syracuse University, Queens College, Rhode Island College, and Lewis and Clark College. He has received awards from the American Psychological Association and the American Association on Mental Deficiency.